Begriffe des Chaos
Chaos der Begriffe

Selbst- und Weltwahrnehmungen der Muslime

Internationales Symposium
Islamische Gemeinschaft Millî Görüş (IGMG)
28. Oktober 2007, Bonn

plural publications

PLURAL Publications GmbH
Colonia-Allee 3 | D-51067 Köln
T +49 221 942240-260 | F +49 221 942240-201
www.plural-publications.eu | info@plural-publications.eu

© PLURAL Publications GmbH
1. Auflage, Köln, Oktober 2016

Design | Satz | Druck
PLURAL Publications GmbH

ISBN: 978-3-944441-06-1

Begriffe des Chaos
Chaos der Begriffe
Selbst- und Weltwahrnehmungen der Muslime

Kargaşanın Kavramları
Kavramların Kargaşası
Müslümanların Benlik ve Dünya Algıları

Concepts of Chaos
Chaotic Concepts
The Muslims' Perceptions of the Self and of the World

Inhalt

Vorwort

Jede Art der inhaltlichen Auseinandersetzung setzt die Frage voraus, weshalb bestimmten Themen überhaupt eine Relevanz zugeschrieben wird. Damit zusammenhängend stellt sich zudem die Frage, wie auf diese Themen Bezug genommen wird und in welcher Form diese erörtert werden. Anstatt gegenwärtig in der Öffentlichkeit debattierte Themen direkt aufzugreifen, sollten hier Antworten auf folgende zwei Fragen gesucht werden: Was sind die Quellen unserer Fragen und wie suchen wir nach Antworten?

Unmittelbarer Gegenstand des Symposiums „Begriffe des Chaos, Chaos der Begriffe. Selbst- und Weltwahrnehmungen der Muslime" waren daher nicht etwa „Islam und Demokratie" oder „Frauenrechte im Islam", sondern vielmehr die Fragen, weshalb diese Konzepte überhaupt in Relation zueinander gesetzt werden und warum uns ihre Gegenüberstellung als Problem erscheint. Die Beispiele ließen sich sicherlich erweitern auf Begriffe wie Universalität, Fortschritt, Zivilgesellschaft, Menschenrechte, Gleichheit, Politik etc. Ziel des Symposiums war, Begriffe und Konzepte hinsichtlich ihrer Entstehung und ihrer Reproduktion innerhalb der islamischen Diskurse zu durchleuchten. Auf diese Weise wurde nicht nur die Korrelation der genannten Begriffe mit dem Islam problematisiert, sondern in gleichem Maße auch die daraus resultierende Suche nach Antworten im „wahren Islam".

Oft wird die Zeit, in der wir – d. h. Muslime und Nichtmuslime – heute leben, mit Merkmalen wie Komplexität,

Kontingenz, Konfusion, Chaos und Krise charakterisiert. Diese Merkmale wiederum schlagen sich nieder in den Begriffen und Konzepten, mit denen wir hantieren, die uns zugleich jedoch mit einer Orientierung bietenden Ideenwelt ausstatten – genauer gesagt: sie uns aufzwingen.

Der Fokus auf die oben skizzierten Fragestellungen sowie die Bestimmung der historischen, kulturellen, sozialen und politischen Faktoren, die bisher die Wahrnehmung von Muslimen geprägt haben, befähigen uns, soweit es der begrenzte Rahmen eines Symposiums zulässt, die theoretischen wie praktischen Wahrnehmungsmuster der im modernen Zeitalter lebenden Muslime ein Stück weit zu dekonstruieren. Der Aufbau des vorliegenden Bandes orientiert sich an dem Ablauf des Symposiums. Nach einer Begrüßung des (ehemaligen) IGMG-Vorsitzenden Yavuz Çelik Karahan, führte Dr. Mustafa Cerić mit seiner Grundsatzrede in das Thema des Symposiums ein. Im Anschluss daran fanden insgesamt fünf Sitzungen mit unterschiedlichen Schwerpunkten statt. Für das Symposium konnten zahlreiche ReferentInnen aus verschiedenen Ländern gewonnen werden. Einige kurze Informationen zu ihnen können Sie den Kurzbiographien am Ende des Bandes entnehmen.

Wir hoffen, mit dem vorliegenden Tagungsband einen Beitrag zum Diskurs über Muslime in Europa geleistet zu haben und bedanken uns recht herzlich bei all unseren Gästen und jenen, die zu der Verwirklichung des Symposiums beigetragen haben.

Kemal Ergün
Köln, September 2016

Eröffnungsrede

Yavuz Çelik Karahan (Deutschland)

Saygıdeğer Misafirlerimiz!

İslam Toplumu Millî Görüş Teşkilatı olarak düzenlemiş olduğumuz bu sempozyuma hoşgeldiniz diyor, hepinizi saygı ve sevgiyle selamlıyorum.

Malumunuz, dünya kamuoyunun dikkati uzun zamandan beri İslam dininin ve Müslümanların üzerine odaklanmış durumda. Hepimiz, gerek gündelik yaşamımızda gerekse medya ve bilimsel yayınlarda, hemen hemen her gün İslam'la ilgili birbirinden farklı tartışmalara tanık oluyoruz. Bu farklılıklar kendini her şeyden önce tartışma esnasında ortaya atılan kavramlarda gösteriyor: "Ilımlı İslam", "radikal İslam", "siyasal İslam", "gelenekçi İslam", "Euro-İslam" bunların sadece birkaçı. Bununla kalmayıp, liberalizm, sivil toplum, demokrasi, tarihsellik, evrensellik, ilerleme, eşitlik, birey, insan hakları, teknoloji, siyaset, devlet, medeniyet gibi birçok diğer kavram ise bir şekilde İslam ile ilintileniriliyor: "İslam'da kadın hakları" veya "İslam ve Batı" şeklindeki ifadelerde olduğu gibi.

Bu durumda dikkatimizi Müslümanların kendisine yönelttiğimizde, belirttiğimiz konuların onların da gündemlerinin en ön sıralarında yer aldığını görüyoruz. Fakat Müslümanların bu konuları tartışırken kullandıkları kavramların arka planını ciddi manada sorgulamadıklarını sanırım burada itiraf edebiliriz. Nitekim her şeyden önce, bu konuları niçin tartıştığımızı ve nasıl ele aldığımızı sorduğumuzda maalesef tatmin edici bir cevap alamamaktayız.

Hâlbuki, merhum Cemil Meriç'in ifadesiyle söyleyecek olursak: "Düşünmeye başlamak kelimeler üzerinde düşünmekle başlar." Şunu unutmamak gerekir ki kullandığımız kavramlar, her şeyden önce kendimize ve dünyaya nereden baktığımızın ifadeleridirler. Onlar kültürel kodlarımızı, daha da önemlisi inanç kodlarımızı ele verirler. Yaşam felsefemiz, değer verdiklerimiz, sevdiklerimiz veya sevmediklerimiz, dünya görüşümüz bu kavramlarla örülüdür. Tek bir cümleyle söyleyecek olursak: Kullandığımız kavramlar kendi iç dünyamızın dışa yansıması, kelimelere dökülmesidir. O hâlde herhangi bir konuda bir şeyler söylemeden önce, kavramlarımızın kendi anlam dünyamızı ne kadar ifade ettiğini iyi düşünmek zorundayız.

Kıymetli Misafirler!

Bugün burada sizlerle beraber kavramlarımızı yeniden gözden geçirmekle aslında kendi benlik, din ve dünya algılarımızı da tartışmaya açmış oluyoruz. Nasıl ele alırsak alalım, "Biz bugüne kadar neler söyledik?" ve "Bugün neler söylüyoruz?" soruları ister istemez, "Biz kimiz?" ve "Nerede duruyoruz?" sorularını ve peşi sıra muhasebesini de beraberinde getirmektedir. Dolayısıyla bu konuları gündeme taşımak, modern dünyada yaşayan biz Müslümanların, içinde yaşadığımız dünyaya karşı bir süredir geliştirmeye çalıştığımız fikrî ve pratik tutumların bir muhasebesi anlamına gelmektedir şüphesiz.

Bir hususun altını çizmeden geçemeyeceğim: Müslümanların kullandıkları kavramları dahi tartışmaya açmaları zayıflığın ve güvensizliğin değil, bilâkis kendilerine olan özgüvenlerinin bir işaretidir. Amacımız, akıp giden gündem karşısında acele ve hazır cevaplar yetiştirmek yerine, doğru soruları sorarak insanları düşünmeye sevk etmektir. Derdimiz, her türlü fikir ve düşüncenin sorgulandığı ve hiçbir görüşün mutlaklık iddia edemediği bir kargaşa ortamında kalıcı şeyler söyleyebilmektir.

Sözlerimi bitirirken hepinize programımıza iştirak etme nezaketi gösterdiğiniz için teşekkür eder, sempozyumumuzun hayırlara vesile olmasını yüce Rabbim'den niyaz ederim.

Allah'ın selamı üzerinize olsun!

Grundsatzrede

Dr. Mustafa Cerić (Bosnien-Herzegowina)

Assalamu Alaikum,

I am very honoured to be invited to take part in this conference. I must tell you that regarding the title of your conference "Concepts of Chaos, Chaos of Concepts" –I don't know whose suggestion it was that you named this conference in this way– I cannot but agree about at least starting to talk about the chaos that we Muslims currently live in, who we are and what we are supposed to do. My lecture will mainly be inspired by this. I don't know how much time I have, but since I am mufti then you have to be patient because when we take the podium, you are just supposed to listen and be quiet. Now, I am using this opportunity to say that Millî Görüş is the organisation that I would like to thank for what they have done for my country, Bosnia and Herzegovina and also for opening this forum for Muslim intellectuals to come and reflect on some of the issues that are important for us, wherever we live. It is very interesting that we are doing this in Bonn and probably it is a good sign that in Europe we can develop some concepts or clear up some of the confusions that we have in our scholarship. Let me then start by saying that you are probably all familiar with the book of the late Sheikh Sheltut, Sheikh'ul-Azhar Rahmetullah, the book about al-Aqidah wa Shari`ah. Sheikh Sheltut wrote this book for the need of lay Muslims. In it, he explains in a very simple way what aqidah is for Muslims, who are not experts like shuyukh al-Azhar and what the

Shari'ah is for lay men –or laïque if you like. Now this focus on aqidah and shari'ah was obvious in the time of Sheltut, which was in the last century. Sheikh Qaradawi recently visited us in Sarajevo for the occasion of the European Council for Fatwas and he delivered a lecture in our mosque in Sarajevo. He was asked the question about what Islam is today and what the state of Muslims is today. He responded by saying that the Islam is aqidah, Shari'ah and khilafah. So, I said to myself, "We have developed now." Sheikh Sheltut was talking only about aqidah and Shari'ah; now Sheikh Qaradawi is talking about khilafah (or imamah or imamet). From these three concepts, i.e. "What is aqidah, what is Shari'ah, what is imamet?" I arrived at the notion that basically we have three main concepts that we are misusing; the meaning of which we do not fully understand. So, let me now try to explain to you why I think this is very important and this is the core of our religion, of our faith.

Aqidah is a personal thing, a personal faith in God. It is your confession. When we say "ashhadu an la ilahe ill'al-lah" we don't say it in plural. We say "ashhadu": I personally witness that there is no god but Allah and I personally witness that the Prophet Muhammed is the messenger of God. So, this is personal and it depends on your personality and your personal ingredients how this aqidah will be. And I think that Muslims do not have a problem with aqidah. We, Muslims, have the simplest aqidah of all religions or dogma or belief. There is no god but Allah and that is very simple. But some Muslims make this aqidah difficult for reasons I don't understand. Anyway, now I don't want to dwell on this particular concept.

What is Shari'ah? If aqidah is personal and individual, Shari'ah is collective. Thus Shari'ah is connected to morals, to morality. And morality is not personal; morality always deals with your relationship with others because personally you can be moral, but it doesn't affect others whether you are personally moral or immoral. But you are affecting others if you are immoral in relationship to others. So, Sharī`ah as much as aqidah is regulating my personal attitudes and my personal view of the world; Sharī`ah is regulating my communal or my collective attitudes towards others. So, Sharī`ah is more of the community or the family. Now, to Sharī`ah I will come back, but let us come to the imamet.

What is imamet? Imamate, imamat or khilafat? This is history. Aqidah and Sharī`ah are transcendental. The idea of aqidah we got from God because he taught us what to say. Sharī`ah is also transcendental in the sense that we have that in the Tawrat, Injil, and the Qur'an. It is a kind of covenant between us and God but imamate or khilafat is left to us. It is the history of our behaviour and our performance. So, we have to contrast aqidah and Sharī`ah, which is about personal belief with Imamate and Khilafat which requires people organise for actual power. We have to see how we perform on the basis of aqidah and Sharī`ah in the history of imamate, and we are the least and most failing in this particular age, in this particular area because the imamate or imamet, khilafat requires organisation, requires sociology, requires the knowledge of how to organise society. I don't know how much time I have but I think it is useful to say that I accept the analysis of Hamid Dabashi, who wrote Authority in Islam. There he applied Max Weber's theory of charisma saying that the Prophet Muhammad (saw) had charisma based on the idea that charisma comes as a result of your breaking norms and laws of the previous society. You are initiating new laws and norms and then you have followers. So, the Prophet Muhammad was charismatic. But Max Weber divides the post-charismatic period into three areas or three directions: routinisation of charisma, perpetuation of charisma and dissemination of charisma. This is what we call sunnah. So, routinisation of charisma is the Sunni business in the history of Muslims; perpetuation of charisma, which is living charisma, is a Shia business; and dissemination of charisma is the Kharijite idea of what imamet is. I believe that the

Sunnis failed to routinise the charisma to endure for a long time. They failed because Sunnis are too secularised. Even though the Shia are a minority, perpetual charisma survived because this living charisma is always alive in the Shia, and the Kharijites are emerging now in more different ways. So, I believe, because of the failure of the Sunnis to establish this institution of khilafat or their failure to continue with the institution of imamet in khilafat in the history, the Shia came with their perpetual charisma. And it is because the Shia could not prevail that we now have in the history of Muslims, the Kharijite logic of the dissemination of charisma. And Europe witnesses that because in Europe no one can put you together because we are all Kharijites in the sense that we do not accept the routinisation of the sunnah, of this charisma being together; and the Shia somehow cannot routinise the charisma in the history context because they always have something up there. My solution is that the Sunnis and Shia have to come together. The Sunnis have to take something of the perpetual charisma from the Shia and the Shia must take from Sunnis the routinisation of the Sunnah so that we win over the Kharijite logic that we live today. This is my proposal.

So, let me then come back to the Sharīʿah and why you see here an introduction to Islamic jurisprudence. Now, I am going to show you the scheme of the development of the Islamic jurisprudence, which is the development of constitution. This is an illustration by a professor. Her name is Asifa Qurayshi. She is a professor at the Madison University in Wisconsin and she is an expert. She is of Pakistani origin. Oh no! Her father was from Iraq, married an American woman who converted to Islam and she is now professor of Islamic law. It is amazing, I spent three days with her in Madison and we discussed the possibility of creating a universal constitution based on the Sharīʿah and motivated by her idea to compare Sharīʿah with the American constitution. And she is teaching exactly that. It was, you know, a surprise for me to have somebody to take the Sharī`ah and to study it in the context of the American constitution. And she came with very interesting results. As a result of her search or research in that area, she came with this scheme to show how Muslims are hypocrites when they talk about implementing Sharī`ah in their daily life and how the West is also hypocritical telling the Muslims, asking them to give up on the Sharī`ah because basically even though some Muslim countries claim that they implement Sharī`ah, they do not implement Sharī`ah. So, there now, let me show this picture and what it looks like.

Now you have mechanisms of Islamic jurisprudence: Sharī`ah, God's law; Qur'an, sunnah. When we go further, this is ijtihad: legal interpretation by private legal schools. Do not forget that Muslim legal schools are very individualistic and you had 500 schools of ijtihad before it became only four Muslim schools –due to the ideological need of the political powers in Baghdad rather than scholarly demand. Analogue reasoning, canons or constitution, public affair –you are familiar with all of these– consensus and other interpretative tools. Fiqh: positive law, pluralistic, legal, equal and so on. And now, we come to fiqh law and let me say that Sharī`ah is not the fiqh or fiqh is not the Sharī`ah. Fiqh is only understanding or the attempt to understand the Sharī`ah. Sharī`ah is always transcendental, it is not terminable, it is perpetual and it is valid even when we don't know what is there. So, we have to understand that. So, these are basically two for six schools. That can be recognised.

Now you can see that this is siyasah and fiqh. The ulama in the classical age were independent of the siyasah. They were intellectuals and scholars. Now, we will see how the ulama became a part of the political system and how they lost their freedom and their dignity. This is why we are where we are today. Now, we can see how the siyasah is coming closer to fiqh, to the ulama. But, still muftis and others were somehow independent in their thinking from the siyasah. There is a difference between mufti and kadi. I am glad that I'm mufti and not kadi because muftis can give opinions but the kadi is responsible for implementing these opinions and he can say any opinion of the mufti there. So, I think this is the richness of the Islamic culture.

Now let's see here: law under the nation state model. I don't need to tell you anything; this is how, I think, today we have the organisation of the so-called Muslim states in which Muslims are a majority. These are the executive order, legislation, case law. They are all basically based on non-Sharī`ah laws even though they claim to be Sharī`ah laws. And the Sharī`ah law and the scholars in Muslim countries are in the corner.

Here the classical Islamic model, there the nation state model today. You can see that legislation in the Muslim countries is based on politics today, not on the principles of Sharī`ah. You see how small a space is left in the model Muslim nation state for the Sharī`ah. You see this is where we are, Millî Görüş, we are in the corner here whereas life goes there without us. Now, classical fiqh was legislative fiqh; singular, uniform, pluralistic. We have to have singular today, uniform; all the ulama know, of course, we need unity, but at what price?

Even though we have the hadith that says "My ummah will not agree in dalal," we have, unfortunately, recently seen that Muslims sometimes do, or that they are silent. There is uniformity in certain things but we, as Muslims, cannot understand why. We have a pluralistic singular; Sharī`ah courts declare the Islamic law as landbinding, non-binding, you see. This is the emergence of siyasi [political] Sharī`ah. This is where we have stopped. I think from here on we have not developed what was started as a political theory of the Muslim state. We stopped there somewhere. We have been reading Jean Jacques Rousseau or Thomas Hobbes and many others because we did not carry on. I believe there is no continuity of Muslim political thought. If you agree with this, you have the right to agree; but if you don't agree, then please contest this and tell me that this is not right.

I believe that this is what classical Islam was, where the ulama and siyasah were living together. Ulama were independent. Now the ulama have re-emerged in the political business, especially Sunni ulama. They have lost their dignity and their authority, and this is why we have this mess. I hope that we will gain our independence in the Sharī`ah and be able to tell the rulers that they should apply certain universal principles based on the Sharī`ah. So, I am closing with this thought reminding you that Islam is aqidah, Sharī`ah and imamet or khilafat. We don't have the time to talk about the imamet; but if we open up the discussion about what imamet is, what khilafat is in the terms of creating a singular or a single Muslim authority in Europe, I think we will do a great service to the ummah as a whole.

Thank you very much for your patience.

Islam and the Problem of Concept Formation in the Study of Religion: The Case of Al-Bīrūnī on "Hinduism"

Dr. Syed Farid Alatas (Singapur)

Introduction

The critique of Eurocentrism and Orientalism in the social sciences and humanities has been directed at the complicity of knowledge in colonialism, academic or intellectual imperialism, and the dominance of American and, to some extent, European academic institutions in most disciplines and fields of study. A specific area illustrating all of these problems is that of the currency and dominance of concepts originating in Western European and American historical and social contexts being applied to other historical and cultural settings. This translation of cultural terms into scientific concepts results in a number of problems in the social sciences. Social scientific concepts originate from cultural terms in everyday language. As such they present problems when brought into scientific discourse and used to talk about areas and periods outside of those of their origins. The result is a distortion of the phenomena that they are applied to. The purpose of this paper is twofold. The first purpose is to explain the process by which cultural terms become social scientific concepts and result in a "loss of meaning" or elision of reality when applied to times and places outside of those of their origin. This is done for the concept of religion as it is applied to Hinduism. The second is to present an alternative construction of Hinduism based on the work of the Muslim scholar, Al-Bīrūnī.

In the first section I discuss the concept of religion as it emerged and developed in the Roman times, charting the changes in meaning over time and its final entry into the conceptual vocabulary of the social sciences. This is followed by a discussion of problems surrounding the definition of religion, with particular focus on the issue of inclusive and exclusive definitions. The next sections focus on problematic constructions arising from the exclusive definition of religion, with illustrations drawn from Islam and Hinduism. I then turn to the question of alternative constructions of Hinduism, attempting here a reconstruction of Al-Bīrūnī's construction of "Hinduism". The concluding section raises the issue of a universal concept of religion.

The Development of the Concept of Religion

The emergence and development of the concept of religion can be seen in a number of historical stages, that is, those of pre-Christian Rome, early Christianity (the Catholic Church), the modern period (Renaissance, Reformation, Enlightenment) and the nineteenth century.

The etymological approach is the least fruitful for our purposes but is, nevertheless, necessary in order to begin to think of the connotations of "religion". "Religion" originates from the Latin *religio*. The three verbs *relegere* (to conscientiously observe), *religari* (binding oneself to one's origin and goal) and *reeligere* (goal) are possible derivations of *religion* and refer to different but converging religious attitudes (Rahner, 1989: 1359).

In pre-Christian Rome, *religio* was a collective term referring to the cultic patterns and ceremonies at the shrine of a god (Smith, 1962: 21). When Rome became

Christian, Christianity became the dominant belief system and all other cults were either absorbed or eliminated. *Religio* in early Christianity was frequently used during the first four centuries but appeared less often from the fifth century on. Prior to that, when Christianity as a religion existed alongside many rivals, the term was applied. However, by the fifth century these rivals were largely eliminated and the term came to be less frequently used (Smith, 1989: 24-25). In fact, there was no need to continue to apply *religio* to Christianity as Christianity was the only legitimate belief, so it was just known as the Church (Matthes, 2000: 56). To the extent that it was used during this period, it had as varied meanings as ritual practices, worship (of God), piety, the bond between God and man, and the structural organization of the Church and its various ecclesiastical levels (Smith, 1962: 25, 26, 29).

In the early modern period, the phrase "Christian religion" came to be used more frequently to refer to Christianity with the appearance of the Christian Platonist, Marsilio Ficino's *De Christiana Religione* in 1474 (Smith, 1962: 33, 36). Greek words in the New Testament were translated into English as "religion" and referred to (i) correct religious observances or worship; (ii) a recognized structure of ethical behaviour; and (iii) obedience to the Christian faith (The Interpreter's Dictionary of the Bible: vol. 4: 32), as opposed to non-Christian worship and behaviour.

But with Luther and the Protestant Reformation *religio* took on an oppositional meaning. *Christiana religio* came to refer to Christian beliefs and a way of life separate from the institution of the Catholic Church. It was oppositional to the clergy, that is, it was the laymans' religion. It was also during this period that *religio* begins to take on a broader meaning closer to the way it is understood today, that is, a system of ideas, beliefs, or doctrine (Smith, 1962: 40), and not just piety, the bond between God and man, or worship. A work that marks this change is Hugo de Groot's *De Veritate Religionis Christianae* (Smith, 1962: 39, n. 107). In addition to this radical shift, there were two other important transformations that *religio* went through. One is its generalization to include non-Christian beliefs and practices and the other is its entry into the social sciences.

In the early days of the history of *religio* the term was applied mainly to Christianity. However, early English translations of the Bible do use *religio* to refer to Judaism as well, although this is held to refer to the outer expressions rather than the inner spirit. This is the sense in which the term is used for Judaism in English translations of the Bible from the fourteenth to seventeenth centuries (Hastings, vol. IV: 225). But *religio* was still far from the more universal notion of religion of which Christianity was just one example.

Matthes (2000: 56) notes that an early proof of the generalization of the concept of religion to belief systems other than Christianity is to be found in Jean Bodin's 1593 work, the *Colloquium Heptaplomeres* (*Colloquium of the Seven about the Secrets of the Sublime*) (Bodin, 1593/1857/1976). This colloquium contains a fictitious discussion between six representatives of various belief systems and is an early instance of inter-religious dialogue in Europe. Three of the representatives, a Catholic, a Lutheran and a Calvinist, by then were traditionally regarded as having *religio*. Bodin also includes a Muslim, a proponent of a "religion of reason" and a "religious universalist" (Matthes, 2000: 56). As Matthes notes, it is very significant that Bodin brought in a Muslim into this debate, even though Islam was widely regarded as wrong belief at best. Matthes makes the very interesting point that the way that this fictitious colloquium was structured clearly demonstrates that Bodin regarded all six belief systems as "religion".

Due to its rather radical position on religion, the work only appeared in published form in 1857.

By the nineteenth century, "religion" in the sense of a community of adherents with institutionalized beliefs and practices and also referring to belief systems other than Christianity was becoming widespread.

Problems in the Definition of Religion

The trajectory of *religio* was such that it began as an inclusive term when it referred to the cults in and around Rome, but remained exclusive when applied solely to Christianity for centuries, and then returns as a more inclusive definition during the nineteenth century. Still, the problem of definition continues to be debated. One of the points of debate concerns the question of inclusive versus exclusive definitions of religion. The debate surrounds the issue of the relative merits and demerits of inclusive and exclusive definitions of religion.

The Inclusive Definition of Religion

Syed Hussein Alatas discusses various problems of the definition of religion, including that of conceptual inflation. This refers to the tendency to generalize or dilute the meaning of a term such that precision and clarity are sacrificed (Alatas, S. H., 1977: 226). Conceptual inflation involves increasing the range of empirical reality to which a particular concept refers but which are not included in people's religious experience. Alatas' argument is as follows. He develops a definition of religion on the basis of enumerative induction. Enumerative induction refers to the exhaustive enumeration of the traits of religion derived from the various dimensions of religious life, that is, the psychological, the social and the philosophical (Alatas, S.H., 1977: 215). He lists the following traits of religion as identified by scholars of religion by way of enumerative induction (215-216):

1. belief in a supernatural being or beings

2. a corresponding invisible order or dimension

3. a personal relationship between humans and the supernatural being or beings

4. specific rites and beliefs sanctioned or required by the supernatural being or beings, such as belief in an afterlife, prayer, etc.

5. the distinction between the sacred and profane in life with corresponding division of activities and objects such as rituals or places of worship

6. belief that the supernatural communicates with humans through human messengers

7. ordering life in harmony with the conception of truth as established by the supernatural being or beings

8. belief that revealed truth supersedes that resulting from human efforts

9. the establishment of a community of believers such that religion informs both individual as well as collective life.

These are what Alatas calls the permanent characteristics of religion which must be distinguished from the variable traits, that is, those traits that are not essential and universal characteristics of religious life and experience (216). Examples of variable traits that he cites are the presence of magic or religions representing a particular nation or group. Apart from enumerating the traits of religion, religion can also be defined in terms of its function such as the integration of group and individual life or the differentiation of action according to notions of right and wrong, good and bad (217). Alatas then points out that the traits and function of religion could be condensed into a single concept, that of meaning.

Were one to condense the traits and function of religion into a single sentence containing a minimum number of concepts one would find the concept of meaning predominant. It is not fear, hope for security in this world or the hereafter, the desire for reward or mere conditioned habit that motivates a genuinely religious person in his devotion: it is the sense that life has a particular meaning, and only one single meaning, which is that provided by his faith. Whatever psychological states flow out in the form of overt religious behaviour, underlying it is always this profound sense of meaning (218).

Religions as they are found in the empirical world and throughout history conform to the above definition of religion, as the definition itself is a result of enumerative induction from the phenomena of religion. The methodology of concept formation is such that the general concept of religion is derived from its inductive base, the total phenomena of particular cases of religion, from which common characteristics, including ideas, overt behaviour, psychological processes, and the hierarchy of significance attached to them within each religion, are selected. This selection determines the constant of our general concept, but before we start selecting we must have a notion of what a general concept should be, which in turn is subject to continual modification by particular cases, so that it cannot avoid being a dynamic concept. It must always be fed from below. If the particular cases remain constant in their fundamentals over a considerable time, a relatively constant general concept, applicable to existing cases, can be derived. Such a concept of religion exists. Such a concept of religion exists and is applicable to all known cases. It is used here to define types of phenomena designated by historical consensus as religious and differing from the type designated as non-religious (Alatas, S.H., 1977: 221-222).

The logic of concept formation in enumerative induction is not circular. It is not that a decision is first made as to what the empirical religions are and then the traits of the general concept are derived from them. These traits may be derived from any particular religion and then found to exist in other belief systems that we designate as religion.

But Alatas notes that the term religion has been erroneously extended to include other phenomena such as "Hitler's Nazism and American Baseball". He also discusses Erich Fromm's conception of religion which includes (i) a set of doctrines, whether theistic or non-theistic; (ii) an attitude (humanitarian, authoritarian); (iii) an outcome of psychological tendencies such as love, masochism, sadism or insecurity; and (iv) a private obsession that takes the form of neurosis such as ancestor worship, a cult of cleanliness, etc. (Fromm, 1950: 29, cited in Alatas, S.H., 1977: 222). This then raises the question of how to distinguish religious from non-religious phenomena (219). If the above traits listed by Fromm are taken as part of the definition of religion it becomes impossible to distinguish religions from naturalistic ways of life (Alatas, S.H., 1977: 222).

Such a loose concept of religion is the result of what Alatas calls conceptual inflation, which he borrowed from Huizinga's Dutch phrase *inflatie der termen*. Huizinga gave the example of the term "Renaissance" which became so general that it lost its value (Huizinga, 1937: 70-71, cited in Alatas, S.H., 1977: 226).

What is required for this conceptual inflation is pluralistic reductionism. Alatas notes that there are two kinds of reductionism. One explains a phenomenon in terms of a single cause, and the other in terms of a number of causes. The latter is termed pluralistic reductionism (Alatas, S.H., 1977: 229). As far as the concept of religion is concerned, it is being pluralistically reduced, as it were, to the characteristics of non-religion. An example would be replacing the idea of the "instinctive search for God" with that of the search for meaning to the environment and the creation of a reified symbol. This is at odds with the phenomenological sense of religion in which God is not a symbol but a reality (Alatas, S. H., 1977: 230). The result of such a reductionism is that the concept of religion is reduced to certain traits to the exclusion of others. The exclusion of other traits renders the concept so general that the distinction between what is usually understood as religion and non-religion is removed. The reason for the conceptual inflation of the concept of religion is that secular humanism rebelled against religion and dispensed with the supernatural, prayer, the holy, and life after death. There is, therefore, resistance to establishing religious phenomena as qualitatively independent and distinct (Alatas, S.H., 1977: 231-232).

The Exclusive Definition of Religion

The opposite of conceptual inflation is conceptual deflation, which takes place when the concept is "diminished in scope, so as to exclude relevant potential content as much as possible. Conceptual deflation is often the result of reductionism (Alatas, S.H., 1977: 227, 229).

Herbrechtsmeier might accuse S. H. Alatas himself of conceptual deflation because the latter includes as a key trait in the definition of religion belief in a supernatural being or beings. Herbrechtsmeier, on the other hand, claims that Buddhism is largely devoid of such a belief in supernatural beings but it has all the other features of religion such as temples, ritual practices, a sacred canon, pilgrimage sites, reverence for saints, and priest-monks (1993: 7). The claim that the Theravada *dharma* (central teachings) is derived from a superhuman Buddha is a distortion of Buddhism because it is not Buddha's being superhuman but his being transcendental, referring to the residing of his transcendental spirit in the teachings or *dharma*, that makes the *dharma* valid (1993: 11).

Herbrechtsmeier suggests that Western scholars often brought in ideas of religion into non-Western contexts that do not fit the experience and understanding of the peoples that they study, resulting in the etic concept of religion not allowing for a empathic and non-distorted understanding of the variety of emic religious phenomena outside of the West. An example is the Western association of religion with worship of supernatural beings (1993: 1).

To the charge that the emic concept of religion is being falsely attributed to Buddhist understandings Alatas would claim that while it may be true that Buddha himself did not preach about a supernatural being, millions of Buddhists in Asia do believe in supernatural beings. In fact, he uses the example of Buddhism to make the point that the basis of enumerative induction by which the concept of religion is derived is empirical reality. In the case of Buddhism, what matters is not what some agnostic Buddhists and Western scholars say about the absence or presence of supernatural beings in Buddhism but rather whether millions of Buddhists in Asia actually understand and practice Buddhism in a way that is consistent with the definition of religion as suggested by Alatas (1977: 222).

What emerges from the above discussion on inclusive and exclusive definitions of religion is the idea that both conceptual inflation and deflation are partly outcomes of the superimposition of Western ideas and experiences of religion onto religious phenomena outside of the West. What is interesting and relevant for our purposes here is the nature of the construction of other "religions" that result from such superimposition. We have already seen how both the concept of religion (as in the conceptual inflation of "religion") as well as the definition of a specific religion (as in the characterization of Buddhism as theistic, as claimed by Herbrechtsmeier) may be outcomes of Western understandings. This raises the crucial question of the nature of such Westernized constructions (of "religion" in general, as well as specific religions) which is what I turn to in the next sections.

The Intellectual Christianization of "Religion"

For this, I draw upon the work of Joachim Matthes (2000). While "religion" meant all beliefs, when European scholars wrote about religion critically, they had in mind Protestantism (religion is opium) or the institutional religion (Catholicism) as opposed to religion of believers (Protestants).

This also applies to the application of "religion" to beliefs other than Christianity. There is an implicit or explicit comparison with Christianity which results in problematic constructions, that is, emic conceptions that are falsely attributed to believers. To understand this, it is necessary to consider what is involved in the logic of comparison.

Logic of comparison is such that the two things to be compared are subsumed under a third unit which is at a higher level of abstraction (Matthes, 2000: 96). For example, apples and pears are subsumed under fruits. This third term is the *tertium comparationis*. The problem arises if the characteristics of the third term are not sufficiently general but are derived largely from one of the units that are being compared.

In the comparison between Christianity and Islam both are subsumed under the third term, religion. The problem with this is that the characteristics of religion are derived from Christianity to begin with. Therefore, the supposedly general scientific concept "religion" is culturally defined by Christianity and Islam is looked at in terms of Christianity rather than compared to Christianity in terms of a general concept "religion".

The danger of the intellectual or what Matthes calls the 'hidden' cultural Christianization of other religions (Matthes, 2000: 98) is the reading into other religions the attributes of Christianity because the comparative dimension of religion was derived exclusively from Christianity. The result is a distortion or loss of meaning.

This is what S. H. Alatas refers to as conceptual deflation, ie. the concept is diminished in scope, reducing the range of empirical reality that it can refer to. When applied to certain realities there is, therefore, a loss of reality (Alatas, 1977: 229). The only difference in the case of intellectual Christianization is that the deflation is not made explicit. The deflated concept is not defined as such. In fact, the assumption is that "religion" is defined in such a manner that it is sufficiently universal to include what in the past were considered non-religions or heathenisms. But because the Christian elements remain dominant, albeit unarticulated, features of the concept or, if having been consciously expunged were unwittingly smuggled back in, the definition of religion is exclusive.

The idea of the intellectual Christianization of "religion" presupposes a more general notion of constructions of which the former is a type. This general notion is based on the critique of Orientalism by Edward Said.

Said describes Orientalism as not just a learned field or discipline, but a "theoretical stage affixed to Europe". The Orientalist, like a dramatist who puts together the drama, constructs images of the Orient in a way that betrays the influence of the history and cultural climate of his society (Said, 1979: 63). Orientalism represents more Western knowledge of the Orient rather than true discourse about the Orient (Said, 1979: 6, 63). Said makes a distinction between early or pre-modern Orientalism and modern Orientalism. Pre-modern Orientalism, formally beginning in 1312 as a result of the establishment of chairs in Arabic, Greek, Hebrew and Syriac at universities in Avignon, Bologna, Oxford, Paris and Salamanca (Said, 1979: 49-50), was articulated and elaborated by prominent European authors such as Ariosto, Milton, Marlowe, Tasso, Shakespeare, Cervantes and others, all of whom helped sharpen the image of the Orient (Said, 1979: 63).

Early Orientalism was not simply ignorant of the Orient, it was characterised by a complex ignorance of the Orient (Southern, 1962: 14, cited in Said, 1979: 55). The image of the Orient was not only far from reality but also complex. The Orient was seen to be hostile to Europe but also weak and defeated, although always a threat, in contrast to a powerful Europe that speaks on her behalf, as when Aeschylus has the Persian queen speak rather than the Persians speaking on their own volition (Aeschylus, 1970, cited in Said, 1979: 57). Said makes a very interesting point about early Orientalism. In the encounter between East and West the Orient neither remains as something completely novel to the Occident nor as something completely well-known. Instead a "new median category emerges, a category that allows one to see new things, things seen for the first times as versions of a previously known thing" (Said, 1979: 58-59). An example of a new thing was Islam, at least to medieval Europeans, which was gradually dealt with by being considered as a fake version of something known, that is, Christianity (Said, 1979: 59). Here Said is speaking of the European Christian view of Islam which developed and spread in poetry, scholarly controversies and popular superstitions (Said, 1979: 61).[1]

My concern is not so much with the Christian or Western views of non-Western religions as such, but with the intellectual Christianization of these "religions", that is, the attribution of Christian-like traits to other belief systems as a result of the application of Christian concept and categories to these belief systems. This can be seen as a special case of the Western view of other religions. Said comes close to discussing this problem when he refers to the analogical constraint that acts on European Christian thinkers. They assumed that "Mohammed was to Islam as Christ was to Christianity" (Said, 1979: 60). In early Orientalism, the Europeans referred to Islam not as Islam

---

1   See also Comfort (1940, cited in Said, 1979: 61, n. 40).

but as Mohammedanism, a consequence of this analogical constraint. With Jesus and Muhammad juxtaposed in that way, the "truth" must be that the latter is a fake, an imposter (Daniel, 1960: 33, cited in Said, 1979: 60). An early observer of Islam in this manner was St. John of Damascus.[2] The Europeans attributed to Islam the intention to deceive by posing as the true religion. Islam could then be rejected on the grounds that it was Christian heresy. This is an instance of the intellectual Christianization of Islam because Islam is not looked at on its own terms, in terms of how it sees itself. Rather, Islam is viewed much like any other Christian heretic claim that had to be rejected by the Church. Islam is first Christianized and then rejected on the grounds that it is fake Christianity.

The late eighteenth and early nineteenth centuries saw the period of the emergence of modern Orientalism. There began to be far greater emphasis on the scientific study of the Orient. This was partly due to the translations of newly discovered Arabic, Sanskrit and Zend texts as a well as the awareness of a new kind of relationship between the Orient and the West, symbolized by the Napoleonic invasion of Egypt in 1798 (Said, 1979: 42-43). Modern Orientalism retained its original features as a thought style founded upon an ontological and epistemological distinction between the Occident and the Orient, which formed an important part of the collective consciousness of European scholars and lay people alike, and which was functional in the domination, restructuring and authorizing of the Orient (Said, 1979: 2-3). This was not unrelated to the fact that Europeans were not just reading, writing and talking about the Orient but were also governing it. Practically all the sciences were complicit in the development of modern Orientalism. The Orient could not represent itself but had to be spoken on behalf of by the West (Said, 1979: 6), as Orientals were irrational, backward and

---

2   See Sahas (1972).

uncivilized. Hence, the "free-floating mythology of the Orient" that went hand-in-hand with more scholarly and scientific research (Said, 1979: 53).

The intellectual Christianization of Islam is found in modern Orientalism as well. Engels had referred to Islam as a fake religion.[3] While Marx and Engels regarded all religions as founded on illusion they nevertheless understood Christianity to be a universal religion while Islam was an Oriental religion.[4] The Orientalist, Duncan Black Mcdonald was of the opinion that Islam was second-order Arian heresy (Mcdonald, 1933: 2, cited in Said, 1979: 63, n. 44).

The Intellectual Christianization of "Hinduism"

What reality is lost? What is the distortion done to belief systems other than Christianity as a result of this intellectual Christianization? Let us consider the case of Hinduism.

According to Smith, Hinduism is a particularly false conceptualization, one that is conspicuously incompatible with any adequate understanding of the religious outlook of the Hindus. Even the term 'Hindu' [an Indian or non-Muslim inhabitant of India] was unknown to the classical Hindus. 'Hinduism' as a concept they certainly did not have" (Smith, 1964: 61, cited in Frykenberg, 1989: 102, n. 3). The term 'Hindu' has its origins in antiquity as the Indo-Aryan name of the river Indus, which is its Greek transliteration (Smith, 1964: 249, n. 46, cited in Frykenberg, 1989: 83)[5]. It is from this usage that the terms 'Hindu' and 'Hinduism' gradually acquired their descriptive and geographical denotations. Muslim scholars such as al-Bīrūnī (A.D. 973-), writing in Arabic, used the term *al-Hind* to refer to the Indian subcontinent, but when they

---

3   Marx and Engels (1953: 96, cited in Alatas, 1977: 234).
4   Marx and Engels (1975: 178).
5   Smith's source is Spiegel (1881, Vol. 1, lines 17-18, A, line 25: 50, 54, 246).

referred to the people of that subcontinent or aspects thereof they were referring to what they considered the indigenous and non-Muslim inhabitants of India. In Persian and Urdu the corresponding geographical term to *al-Hind* was *Hindustân*. Things *Hindustānī* referred to whatever that was indigenous to India and non-Muslim (Frykenberg, 1989: 84). The English 'Hindu' probably derived from the Persian. The term "Hindu" appears in the *Gaudiya Vaisnava* texts of the sixteenth century (O'Connell, 1973: 340-3, cited in Frykenberg, 1989: 84), probably as a result of Muslim influence. The usage here is consistent with that in the Muslim texts of the premodern Arabs and Persians. Even in the modern period, this negative definition of Hinduism is found as evident in the Hindu Marriage Act. The Act defines a Hindu, among other things, as one "who is not a Muslim, Christian, Parsi or Jew by religion..." (Derret, 1963: 18-19).

The terms 'Hindu' and 'Hinduism' in reference to religion, and a unitary one at that, were for the most part, a modern development. In the eighteenth century they began to be used to denote an Aryan, Brahmanical or Vedic-based high culture and religion by European Orientalists such as Halhed, Jones and Müller (Frykenberg, 1989: 85-86). It is this usage that was adopted by the early Indian nationalists themselves like Ramohun Roy, Gandhi and Nehru (Frykenberg, 1989: 86). This 'new' religion was founded on the ontology and epistemology contained in the *Varnāsramadharma* and encompassed the entire cosmos, detailing as part of its vision a corresponding stratified social structure (Frykenberg, 1989: 86).

What is important in these developments as far as the intellectual Christianization of Indian beliefs systems is concerned is that (i) the belief systems of the inhabitants of the Indian subcontinent (excluding Muslims, Jews, Christians and Parsis) came to be regarded as religion; (ii) these beliefs systems were seen to constitute a single religion; and (iii) they were founded on a system of Brahmanical doctrines based on the *Catur-Veda* (Four Vedas) (Frykenberg, 1989: 86). It is in these senses that character-istics of Christianity were read into Indian beliefs.

Gradually, the newly christened Hinduism also came to encompass the 'low' tradition or what is nowadays re-ferred to as 'popular', 'temple', 'bhakti', 'village', or 'tribal' Hinduism (Frykenberg, 1989: 87).

This is a construction at odds with indigenous think-ing and experience as there was never such a thing as a sin-gle all-encompassing religion (or *dharma*, for that matter) called Hinduism or any other name that can be traced to the Vedas and that characterize the beliefs of the non-Muslim, non-Jewish, non-Christian, non-Parsi population of India. Instead, what happened was a process of reification, that is, an ideal type of the 'Hindu' religion was constructed and assumed to be a description of the real Indian society. As Deshpande suggests, this is a "case of simulated identity which over the years has been accepted as true identity" (Deshpande, 1985, cited in Frykenberg, 1989: 101).

Looking at South Indian examples, Frykenberg tells us how this happened in practical terms beginning in the nineteenth century. Modern Hinduism is a form of corpo-rate and organized and 'syndicated' religion which arose in south India and by which highly placed and influen-tial groups of Brahmans, supported by Brahmanized Non Brahmans, did most of the defining, the manipulating, and the organizing of the essential elements of what gradual-ly became, for practical purposes, a dynamic new religion. Moreover, this process of reification, this defining and or-ganizing of elements which they did, occurred with the col-laboration, whether witting or unwitting, with those who governed the land (Fykenberg, 1989: 89).

This was facilitated by the process of centraliza-tion, rationalization, and bureaucratization of information (Dykes, 1854: 232, cited in Frykenberg, 1989: 89), which had two bases. One was the interaction between local officials and the rulers, examples of which are the patronage of cultural events and the policy with respect to temples and their administration. The latter entailed the collection and preservation of information (historical, archaeological, artistic) (Frykenberg, 1989: 89, 91, 92, 94) that served to concretize a concept that was gradually developing in the minds of colonial scholars and administrators, and local elites. The other refers to movements outside of the state structure that acted as lobbies and pressure groups that sought to bring about changes to the structure in line with their aspirations or which acted to counter Christian proselytization (Frykenberg, 1989: 95-96).

The dangers of adopting a purely formal definition of Hinduism without taking into account the historical background of the genesis of the concept is illustrated in Sharma's article. Sharma adopts the reified category of 'Hinduism' and problematizes it in terms of the diversity of beliefs and practices that the term is supposed to refer to and the outliers and exceptions that are difficult to capture under existing definitions (Sharma, 1986). While this is certainly part of the problem, little can be achieved concerning the definition of Hinduism without considering the historical development of the concept as well as the social and political factors that account for its formation. As such, his approach is not very sociological, contrary to what the title of his paper might suggest.

In the previous section it was suggested that the intellectual Christianization of "religion" is a special case of the application of an exclusive definition of religion. The exclusivity of the definition is smuggled into the concept unwittingly. The result is a specific type of construction of religion determined in the first place by the elements smuggled into the concept of religion to begin with. I have argued that the elements smuggled into the understanding of Islam and "Hinduism" are derived from Christianity.

The application of a universal concept of religion would not result in such constructions of individual religions because the elements that make up the universal concept of religion are derived from all religions, apply to all of them with varying degrees of significance and are, therefore, neutral, in the sense that one is not led by the very concept of religion to read into a particular religion the traits of another. The neutrality of the universal concept of religion would extend to all related concepts in the study of religion. A universal concept of religion implies neutrality for all other concepts applied in the description and analytical study of religion. The reverse is also true. A non-universal concept of religion, such as an exclusive one, would render all other concepts in the study of religion non-universal.

Therefore, the use of the conceptual vocabulary of one religion to talk about another religion is not in itself a problem if the concept of religion in operation is the universal one. For example, in the sociology of religion concepts such as sect and denomination are defined in terms of another concept, that of the church. Since the idea of the church as a religious organization does not exist in other religions, the use of concepts like denomination and sect for other religions runs the risk of resulting in an intellectual Christianization of these religions. In Islam, for example, the terms denomination and sect cannot be used to refer to the Sunni and Shi'ite branches of Islam as they both imply a certain relationship vis a vis a church, which is non-existent in Islam. The problem lies in the non-universality of terms like sect and denomination.

But it cannot be said that the conceptual vocabulary of one religion cannot be sufficiently universalized such that it can be applied to another religion without intellectually constructing that religion after its own image. For this reason, it is interesting to examine the Muslim scholar, Al-Bīrūnī's attempt to understand the religion(s) of India.

Al-Bīrūnī's Intellectual and Social Context

Abu Rayhan Muhammad ibn Ahmad al-Bīrūnī (973-1048) was born in the city of Khwārazm (modern Khiva) in what is today known as Uzbekistan, but during his youth was part of the Iranian Samanid Empire. He spent his early years under the patronage of various rulers until finally becoming part of the court of Mahmud Ghaznavi (979-1030), the ruler of an empire that included parts of what is now known as Afghanistan, Iran and northern India. Al-Bīrūnī went to India with the troops of Mahmud and remained there for many years. During this time, he studied Sanskrit, translated a number of Indian religious texts, and conducted research on Indian religions and their doctrines. Al-Bīrūnī was the first Muslim and probably the first scholar to provide a systematic account of the religions of India from a sociological point of view. Furthermore, his work is considered to be a vital source of knowledge of Indian history and society in the eleventh century, providing details of the religion, philosophy, literature, geography, chronology, astronomy, customs, laws and astrology of India.

Typical of the great scholars of his period, Al-Bīrūnī was multitalented, being well-versed in physics, metaphysics, mathematics, geography and history. He wrote a number of books and treatises. Apart from his *Kitāb ma li al-hind* (*The Book of What Constitutes India*), he also wrote *Al-Qanun al-Masudi* (on astronomy and trigonometry), *Al-Athar al-Baqia* (on ancient history and geography), *Kitab al-Saidana* (Materia Medica) and *Kitab al-Jawahir* (*Book of Precious Stones*). His *Al-Tafhim-li-Awail Sina'at al-Tanjim* gives a summary of mathematics and astronomy. His important work sociologically speaking is his *Kitāb mā li al-Hind* in which he presents a study of Indian religions. Al-Bīrūnī died in 1048 A.D. at the age of 75.

The history of central Asia during the tenth and eleventh centuries provides an important backdrop for the understanding of al-Bīrūnī's intellectual development. He was born in the environs (Persian, *bīrūn)* of Kāth, one of the two main cities of Khwārazm, the other being Jurjāniyya. The title of Khwārazmshāh had been held for a long time by the ruler of Kāth. But in 995 the ruler of Jurjāniyya killed his suzerain and appropriated the title for himself. During the civil war, al-Bīrūnī fled the area for a few years. Various dynasties that once flourished around Khwārazm, such as the Sāmānids to the south-east, the Buwayhids to the west, and the Ziyārid state in-between were gradually absorbed by the Ghaznavids under the leadership of Sultan Mahmūd in central Afghanistan by 1020. During his flight and after it is likely that al-Bīrūnī lived in places such as Rayy (near modern Tehran), Bukhara and Gurgān. In Bukhara he met the famed physician and philosopher, Ibn Sīnā (Avicenna). By 1022, Sultan Mahmūd had conquered large parts of India including Waihand, Multan, Bhatinda, and the Ganges valley up to near Benares. It was during this time that al-Bīrūnī developed an interest in Indian society, living in an empire that conquered large areas of the Indian subcontinent and having the opportunity to travel and take up residence there (Kennedy, 1970).

Al-Bīrūnī's Construction of the Religions of India

Abū al-Rayhān Muhammad bin Ahmad al-Bīrūnī (362 /973 – 445/1048) aimed to provide a comprehensive account of the civilization of India, including the religion, philosophy, literature, geography, science, customs and laws of the Indians. This section concentrates on al-Bīrūnī's construction of the religions of India.[6]

The work of al-Bīrūnī that can be considered as sociological is his study of India. His *Kitāb mā li al-hind* (*The Book of What Constitutes India*) aimed to provide a

---

6   I consult both the original Arabic, the Kitāb fī tahqīq mā li al-hind li al-hind (al-Bīrūnī, A.H.1377/A.D.1958[A.D.c1030] as well as Sachau's English translation, Alberinu's India (Sachau, 1910). Dates in brackets indicate the year in which the work was written. Unless otherwise stated, all quotations in English are taken from Sachau's translation.

comprehensive account of what he called "the religions of India and their doctrines". This included the religion, philosophy, literature, geography, science, customs and laws of the Indians. Of special interest to sociology is al-Bīrūnī's construction of the religions of India. Al-Bīrūnī considered what we call "Hinduism" as religion centuries before Europeans recognized Hinduism as not mere heathenism.

In attempting a reconstruction of al-Bīrūnī's construction of "Hinduism" it is necessary to point out that it is inadequate to rely on Sachau's English translation of the Arabic original. The translation, which was undertaken in the late nineteenth century, reads into Arabic terms, nineteenth century European ideas about what Hinduism was. For example, in his preface in the Arabic original al-Bīrūnī refers to "the religions of India" *(adyān al-hind)* (Al-Bīrūnī, 1377/1958[c1030]: 4) while this is translated by Sachau as "the doctrines of the Hindus" (Sachau, 1910: 6), leading one to assume that al-Bīrūnī conceived of a single religion called Hinduism. As we shall see, this was not the case.[7]

We begin our reconstruction of al-Bīrūnī's construction of the religions of India with the title of his work: *Kitāb al-Bīrūnī fī tahqīq ma li al-hind min maqbūlat fī al-`aql aw mardhūlat.* This can be translated as *The Book of What Constitutes India as derived from Discourse which is Logically Acceptable or Unacceptable.* As noted by Sachau (1910: xxiv), al-Bīrūnī's method was to allow Indians to speak in order to present Indian civilization as understood by Indians themselves (Sachau, 1910: 25; al-Bīrūnī, 1377/1958[c1030]: 19).[8] Al-Bīrūnī quotes extensively from Sanskrit texts which he had either read himself or which were communicated to him.[9]

---

7   In fact, a study of Sachau's translation may be more a study of the intellectual Christianization of the religions of India than of al-Bīrūnī's work on India.
8   For more on al-Bīrūnī's method see Jeffery (1951).
9   On al-Bīrūnī's knowledge of Sanskrit, see Chatterji (1951) and Gonda (1951).

The second chapter of the *Tahqīq ma li al-hind* was translated by Sachau as "On the Belief of the Hindus in God", whereas the Arabic original has it as "On their Beliefs in God, Praise be to Him". Moreover, the term Hindu does not appear in the Arabic text and the term "*hind*" does not have religious connotations. Sachau writes "the Hindu religion" in his translation (Sachau, 1910: 50), whereas the Arabic original has no equivalent (al-Bīrūnī, 1377/1958 [c1030]: 38).

The account of the creed of the Indians begins in chapter two with an exposition of their belief in God, by which al-Bīrūnī means the same God that is worshipped by Jews, Christians and Muslims. The exposition begins with an account of the nature of God, with reference to his speech, knowledge and action (Sachau, 1910: 27-30; al-Bīrūnī, 1377/1958[c1030]: 20-22).

We are then told that this is an account of the belief in God among the elite. Here al-Bīrūnī is making a distinction between ideas associated with a high tradition and ideas held by the common people, as far as the conception of God is concerned (Sachau, 1910: 31-32; al-Bīrūnī, 1377/1958[c1030]: 23-24).

What we get so far is a picture of a monotheistic religion based on a determinate number of books, the *Patañjali*, *Veda* and *Gita* (Sachau, 1910: 27, 29; al-Bīrūnī, 1377/1958[c1030]: 20-21). The Veda was "sent down" to Brahma (*anzalahu ʿalā brāhma*) (Sachau, 1910: 29; al-Bīrūnī, 1377/1958[c1030]: 21), which Al-Bīrūnī understands as the First Power (*al-quwwah al-awwalī*) (Sachau, 1910: 94; al-Bīrūnī, 1377/1958[c1030]: 71). Al-Bīrūnī draws an analogy between the Christian trinity and the three forces of Brahma, Narayana (second force) and the Rudra (third force). The unity of these three forces is called Vishnu, sometimes called the middle force and sometimes conflated with the first force (Sachau, 1910: 94).

Sociologically speaking, a distinction has to be made between the abstract, metaphysical ideas of the high tradition and the literalist, anthropomorphic ideas of the common people.

Al-Bīrūnī is, therefore, referring to a specific Vedic-Sanskritic religion that revolved around the worship of Brahma, which today in retrospect is often seen as a branch or sect within Hinduism, and which was historically a minor tradition among the more major traditions of Vaisnavism, Saivism and Saktism (Klostermaier, 1989: 53). Al-Bīrūnī refers to the tradition around Brahma as a dharma. Dharma refers to, among other things, a system of socio-ethical laws and obligations, including a system of social classification based on the division of society into varnas (castes) (Klostermaier, 1989: 46).

To the extent that the Islamic concept, *dīn*, approximates "religion", Al-Bīrūnī would have understood dharma as religion as he translates dharma as *dīn* (al-Bīrūnī, 1377/1958[c1030]: 30; Sachau, 1910: 40).

In fact, this seems to be the only religion of Hind that is identified by Al-Bīrūnī. He does identify other dharma such as Vaisnavism, Saivism and Saktism (referred to in Sanskrit as *sampradāya*), although he does recognize the existence of other religions in India, that is, religions other than Islam, Judaism and Christianity.

Furthermore, it is clear from a survey of the chapters of the *Tahqīq ma li al-hind* that by a religion of India (*dīn al-hind*), Al-Bīrūnī meant something like the total consciousness of the community that saw itself as worshippers of a deity or group of deities that extended beyond theology and encompassed the various branches of knowledge that are not seen by modern sociology to be part of religion. These include theology, philosophy, literature, metrology, geography, astronomy, chronology, and the study of manners and customs.

The Relevance of Al-Bīrūnī to the Contemporary Study of Religion

Al-Bīrūnī's studies on Indian religions are important for four principal reasons. First is that he pioneered the comparative study of religion. Al-Bīrūnī was extremely versatile as a scholar. In his work in the exact sciences such as in his *Kitâb al-Jawâhir (Book of Precious Stones)*, he was an experimental scientist. But he was well aware that such methods were not suitable for the study of religion and, therefore, employed a comparative approach in his study of India. For example, when he makes the distinction between the abstract, metaphysical ideas of the elite and the anthropomorphic ideas of the masses, he clarifies that this dichotomy is to be found among the ancient Greeks, Jews, Christians and Muslims (Sachau, 1910: 24, 111). In other words, the dichotomy is a universal tendency found in all religions.

Second, his work on India is an example of an early sociological study conscious of the necessity for objectivity. Al-Bīrūnī was an impartial observer of Indian society. This can be seen from the full title of his study: *Kitāb al-Būrīnī fī tahqīq ma li al-hind min maqbūlat fī al-`aql aw mardhūlat*, that is, *The Book of What Constitutes India as derived from Discourse which is Logically Acceptable or Unacceptable*. Al-Bīrūnī's approach was to make assessments based on what was logically acceptable. He was fully aware of the need to refrain from making value judgments about Indian religions from an Islamic perspective. He attempted to present Indian civilization as understood by Indians themselves (Sachau, 1910: 25; al-Bīrūnī, 1377/1958[c1030]: 19). Al-Bīrūnī quotes extensively from Sanskrit texts, which he had either read himself or which were communicated to him.

Third, al-Bīrūnī's work on India is important from a methods point of view because it contains ideas pertinent to social statistics, applied social research, and the issue of numerical evidence (Boruch, 1984). These come under the categories of errors in information, data sharing, the limits of knowledge, and statistics. On errors in information, he was concerned with fixing limits to guesswork and the problems of translation as he relied greatly on Sanskrit sources (Boruch, 1984: 826). He also raised the problem of response bias that arises from ethnocentrism, lying, corroboration, the question of the validity of information (Boruch, 1984: 828-30), and the types of misrepresentations.

On data sharing, al-Bīrūnī was critical of those who resisted doing so, saying that the Indians "are by nature niggardly in communicating that which they know, and they take the greatest possible care to withhold it from men of another caste among their own people, still much more, of course from any foreigner" (Sachau, 1910: 22, cited in Boruch, 1984: 836). On the limits of knowledge, he listed various impediments such as knowledge of languages, carelessness of scribes, a metrical system of writing, and religious insularity (Boruch, 1984: 837). On statistical technique, Boruch notes that although al-Bīrūnī was obviously not familiar with concepts of relative frequency distribution, there is an attempt to articulate an embryonic notion of that when he discusses rare events (Boruch, 1984: 838).

In cautioning us against the various types of lies and misrepresentations, al-Bīrūnī refers to the example of the critics of the Mu'tazila school of theology in Islam. He once called upon a scholar by the name of Abū Sahl 'Abd al-Mun'im Ibn 'Alī Ibn Nūh al-Tiflīsī, who spoke of the misrepresentation of the Mu'tazila school. According to the Mu'tazila, God is omniscient and, therefore, has no knowledge (in the way that man has knowledge). The misrepresentation is that God is ignorant! (Sachau, 1910: 5). It is the same scholar who urged al-Bīrūnī to write a work on the religions of India because of the misrepresentations of India that were found in contemporary works among Muslims (Sachau, 1910: 6-7).

Also on methods, al-Bīrūnī makes an interesting case for hearsay as opposed to eyewitness. We are used to thinking of eyewitness accounts as more reliable than necessary. Al-Bīrūnī concurs when he says that " the eye of the observer apprehends the substance of that which is observed, both in the time when and the place where it exists, whilst hearsay has its peculiar drawbacks" (Sachau, 1910: 3). However, he notes that had it not been for the drawbacks, hearsay would be preferable to eyewitness. The reason for this is that "the object of eye-witness can only be *actual* momentary existence, whilst hearsay comprehends alike the present, the past, and the future, so as to apply in a certain sense both to that which *is* and to that which is *not...*" (Sachau, 1910: 3). In this sense, al-Bīrūnī notes, written tradition is a type of hearsay and the most preferable, observing that if a report regarding an event were not contradicted by logic or physical laws, then its truth or falsity depends on the "character of the reporters, who are influenced by the divergency of interests and all kinds of animosities and antipathies between the various nations" (Sachau, 1910: 3).

While it is true that his study was narrow in that his sources were mainly textual, what is interesting from the sociological standpoint is the definition of *dīn* (plural, *adyān*), the complexity of which is lost when translated into the modern "religion". This then raises the question as to whether al-Bīrūnī imposed an Islamic conception of religion onto his Indian data or derived this broad conception from his Indian textual sources or informants. This issue has so far not been dealt with by scholars of al-Bīrūnī or of Hinduism.

It has been noted that al-Bīrūnī utilized Muslim categories in his study of Indian thought. As Lawrence suggests, the introductory chapters on theology and philosophy of the *Kitîb mî li al-hind* suggests an organizational principle and selection criteria based on the Islamic understanding of God (Lawrence, 1978: 6). However, this cannot be seen as an imposition of Muslim categories as al-Bīrūnī did not read Islamic meanings into the religions of the Indians. It is interesting that al-Bīrūnī's translator, Edward C. Sachau, observed that al-Bīrūnī's method was not to speak himself "but to let the Hindus speak, giving extensive quotations from their classical authors" (Sachau, 1910: xxiv), while Sachau himself does not always allow al-Bīrūnī to speak when he reads modern European meanings into al-Bīrūnī's Arabic text.

Fourth, al-Bīrūnī had a universal conception of *dîn*, which he applies to religions other than Islam, at a time when the Latin *religio* was only applied to Christianity. At the same time, al-Bīrūnī does not intellectually or culturally Islamize the religions of the Indians by reading into the Indian material an Islamic model or Islamic meanings.

References

Aeschylus, *The Persians*, Anthony J. Podleck, trans., Engelwood Cliffs, N. J. Prentice-Hall.

Alatas, Syed Hussein. 1977. *The Myth of the Lazy Native: A study of the image of the Malays, Filipinos and Javanese from the 16ᵗʰ to the 20ᵗʰ century and its function in the ideology of colonial capitalism*. London: Frank Cass.

Alatas, Syed Hussein. 1977. "Problems of Defining Religion", *International Social Science Journal* 29(2): 213-234.

al-Bīrūnī, Abū al-Rayhān Muhammad bin Ahmad. 1377/1958[c1030]. *Kitāb al-Bīrūnī fī tahqīq ma li al-hind min maqbūlat fī al-`aql aw mardhūlat*, Hyderabad: Majlis Da'irāt al-Ma`ārif al-Uthmāniyyah.

Bodin, Jean. 1593/1857/1976. *Colloquium of the Seven about Secrets of the Sublime (Colloquium Heptaplomeres de Rerum Sublimium Arcanis Abditis)*. Translated with an introduction by Marion Leathers Daniels Kuntz Princeton University Press.

Chatterji, Suniti Kumar. 1951. "Al-Bīrūnī and Sanskrit", in Iran Society, *Al-Bīrūnī Commemoration Volume A.H. 362 – A.H. 1362*, Calcutta: Iran Society, pp. 83-100.

Comfort, William Wistar. 1940. "The Literary Role of the Saracens in the French Epic", *PMLA* 55: 628-659.

Daniel, Norman. 1960. *Islam and the West: The Making of an Image*, Edinburgh: Edinburgh University Press.

Derret, J.D.M. 1963. *Introduction to modern Hindu law*, Oxford: Oxford University Press.

Deshpande, G. P. 1985. "The plural tradition", *Seminar* 313: 23-25.

Dykes, J.B.W. 1854. *Salem, an Indian collectorate*, Madras.

Fromm, Erich. 1950. *Psychoanalysis and Religion*, New Haven: Yale University Press.

Frykenberg, Robert Eric. 1989. "The Emergence of Modern 'Hinduism' as a Concept and as an Institution: A Reappraisal with Special Reference to South India", in Günther-Dietz

Gonda, J. 1951. "Remarks on Al- Bīrūnī's Quotations from Sanskrit Texts", in *Al-Bīrūnī Commemoration Volume A.H. 362 – A.H. 1362*, Calcutta: Iran Society, pp. 111-118.

Hastings, James. ed. 1902. *A Dictionary of the Bible Dealing with Its Language, Literature, and Contents Including the Biblical Theology*, 4 vols., Edinburgh: T & T Clarke.

Herbrechtsmeier, William. 1993. "Buddhism and the Definition of Religion: One More Time", *Journal for the Scientific Study of Religion* 32(1): 1-18.

Huizinga, J. 1937. *De Wetenschap der Geschiedenis*, Haarlem: Tjenk Willink.

1962. *The Interpreter's Dictionary of the Bible: An Illustrated Encyclopedia Identifying and Explaining All Proper Names and Significant Terms and Subjects in the Holy Scriptures, including the Apocrypha: with Attention to Archaeological Discoveries and Researches into the Life and Faith of Ancient Times*, 4 vols, New York: Abingdon Press, vol. 4, p. 32.

Jeffery, A. 1951. "Al-Bīrūnī's Contribution to Comparative Religion", *Al-Bīrūnī Commemoration Volume A.H. 362 – A.H. 1362*, Calcutta: Iran Society, pp. 125-160.

Kennedy, E. S. (1970). "Al-Bīrūnī", in Charles Coulston Gillispie, editor in chief, *Dictionary of Scientific Biography*, vol. 1, New York: Charles Scribner's Sons, pp. 147-158.

Klostermaier, Klaus K. (1989) *A Survey of Hinduism*, Delhi: Munshiram Manoharlal.Marx, Karl and Frederick Engels. 1953. *Selected Correspondence*, Moscow:Foreign Languages Publishing House.

Marx, Karl and Frederick Engels. 1975. *On Religion*, Moscow: Progress Publishers.

Matthes, Joachim. 2000. "Religion in the Social Sciences: A Socio-Epistemological Critique", *Akademika* 56: 85-105.

O'Connell, Joseph T. 1973. "Gaudiya Vaisnava symbolism of deliverance from evil". *Journal of the American Oriental Society* 93(3): 340-343.

Rahner, Karl. 1989. *Encyclopedia of Theology: The Concise* Sacramentum Mundi, New York: Crossroads.

Sachau, Edward C. (trans.) 1910. *Alberinu's India: An account of the religion, philosophy, literature, geography, chronology, astronomy, customs, laws and astrology of India about AD 1030*, Delhi: Low Price Publications.

Said, Edward. 1979. *Orientalism*, New York: Vintage Books, 1979.

Sahas, D. J. 1972. *John of Damascus on Islam*, Leiden.

Sharma, Arvind. 1986. "What is Hinduism: a sociological approach", *Social Compass* 33(2-3): 177-183.

Smith, Wilfred Cantwell. 1962. *The Meaning and End of Religion: A Revolutionary Approach to the Great Religious Traditions*, London: SPCK.

Sontheimer & Hermann Kulke, eds., *Hinduism Reconsidered*, New Delhi: Manohar Publishers, pp. 82-107.

Southern, R. W. 1962. *Western Views of Islam in the Middle Ages*, Cambridge, M.A.: Harvard University Press.

Spiegel, Fr. 1881. *Die Altpersischen Keilinschriften, im Grundtext mut Übersetzung, Grammatik und Glossar*, Leipzig.

Comment

Dr. S. Parvez Manzoor (Schweden)

In his paper, Syed Farid Alatas examines one of the pivotal concepts of the modernist worldview, namely religion, and discovers that in its current definitions and interpretations it carries an implicit, though hopefully dispensable, bias towards Christianity. His historical inquiry further yields insights into the ideological parameters of the modern conception of 'religion' which are quite relevant to Muslim self-reflection. Highlighting Albiruni's earlier attempts to 'construct' Hinduism through the consciousness of Islam, Alatas points towards alternative paths to greater conceptual clarity in the study of Comparative Religions. In so doing, Alatas succeeds in showing us another, gentler face of Islam. While the contact in the West, between Islam and Europe, may reveal a sad tale of strife and confrontation, the South-East Asian experience of Islam and the native traditions is one of cohabitation and co-existence, indeed of synthesis and symbiosis.

Alatas's paper is well-written and well-documented. He argues his case with proper academic rigour and manages to keep the polemical impulse under control. It is my good fortune, and heartfelt joy, to commend him on his creative effort. I am confident that his paper will receive due recognition among his academic peers and will stimulate an informed debate on the insights that his study provides. However, since this inquiry relates to the wider ideological debates of our days, issues which are also the focus of attention in this symposium, I'll restrict my brief comments to the more general meta-theoretical concerns of this debate.

'Religion' as the Foundational Myth of Secularism

One of the distinguishing marks of the classical 'Islamic' civilization, according to a modern scholar, was its science of comparative religions, 'the likes of which was not found before[1].' He continues: 'We possess in Arabic comprehensive books about the tenets and beliefs of all the then known denominations, sects, philosophical schools and systems of thought, Muslim and non-Muslim, ancient and modern.' A comparison of Shahrastani's pioneering study, *kitab al-millal wa nahal* (The Book of Religions and Beliefs), 'with its detailed, well informed and remarkably unbiased accounts', with the Greek and Latin texts related to Judaism makes him confess that 'between Tacitus and Shahrastani, 'humanity had made a great leap forward.[2]' He further opines that in order to obtain authoritative information about Judaism, Tacitus merely had to ask any member of the Jewish community. 'But he and his Greek masters, whom he copied, lacked the spirit of research and scientific responsibility needed for the task. How different was Shahrastani, who took pains to study in detail and to describe objectively such sects as the Persian dualists, the Manichaeans and the followers of Mazdak, all of whom were, of course, anathema to him from the view of religion.[3]' Another great scholar in this tradition, whom Alatas also takes as illustrative of the Muslim approach to religion, was of course, Al-Biruni[4].

1 Goitein, S.D.: Studies in Islamic History and Institutions. Leiden (Brill), 1968. P 67.
2 *ibid.*
3 *ibid.*
4 Another study that explores Ibn Hazm's *Kitab al-Fasl fi'l Milal wa'l Ahaw' wa'l-Nahl* is by Ghulam Haider Aasi: *Muslim Understanding of Other Religions.* IIIT & Islamic Research Institute, Islamabad, 1999.

Prof. Goitein's remarks raise a number of questions and observations that are all pertinent to Alatas's paper and relevant to our theme today. The first point is that, the Muslim scholars' understanding of 'religion' was 'sociological', in that they chose 'community' as the unit of their study. The best way to learn about other religions is to study a *milla*, a 'faith community', to examine what it professes and proscribes, and what it practices. Religion represents, in this sense, *tradition*, a collective and cumulative enterprise in history. It binds the individual to a community, as the Latin term also suggests. However, we must also underline that the most paramount and seminal term for religion, *din*, alludes to a transcendent realm: it relates Man - both the individual human soul and the entire human community - to God. Islamic vision in other words affirms both transcendence and history. It is this simultaneous allegiance to transcendence and history, to faith and to community, which creates such an impasse in any conversation between the ideologues of modernity and those of 'Islamism'. (I am of course suggesting that 'Islamism' as *ideology* is not Islam as *tradition*[5]. In fact, in adjusting to the pressures of modernity, Islamism has acquired all the attributes of modernity, namely, renunciation of transcendence, idolization of history, and even predilection for nihilism[6].) Any quest for conceptual clarity thus requires that we pay greater attention to the metaphysical *Urgrund* in which our terms of debate are embedded. We must not reify faith and make history as the be-all and end-all of the human condition.

---

5   Cf: 'Islam is neither a distinctive social structure nor a heterogeneous collection of beliefs, artefacts', customs, and morals. It is a *tradition.' The Idea of an Angthropology of Islam.* Center for Contemporary Arab Studies, Georgetown University, Washington, 1986. P. 14.

6   Gray, John: *AL-QAEDA and what it means to be Modern.* London, Faber and Faber, 2003. Cf. also our review, 'Faith beyond the Messianic Violence of Terror and Empire', in *The Muslim World Book Review*, 25:2 (Winter 2005), pp. 6-17.

Someone who has studied the general metaphysical turn from the transcendental to the positivist modes of perception and articulation that is the landmark of modern consciousness is Wilfred C Smith. As Smith is also the focus of Alatas's attention, something concerning his work and ideas is not out of place in this comment. Smith, it is worth recalling had excessive contacts with Muslims. He not only taught at the 'missionary' Forman Christian College, Lahore, but also authored a number of highly incisive and critical studies of contemporary Islam[7]. As a phenomenologist looking at the problem of religious pluralism, however, Smith's foremost concern in later years was with 'world-theology'[8]. Needless to say, W C Smith is a courteous and non-polemical writer who has interacted both critically and creatively with the Islamic tradition and even acquired his seminal insights (the main thesis of *Faith and Belief*, for instance) through this contact. Smith's main argument, as elaborated in *The Meaning and End of Religion*, must be seen in this light. It is the reification of faith, the historicisation of transcendence as it were, that is the focus of his theological inquiry. In the historical development of the term 'Islam', Smith notices a significant semantic shift: From its original meaning as 'submission to God's will', an act for the acquisition of faith, 'Islam' – an abstract noun signifying search - came to denote the consequence of that act and the result that faith. It became an object and a phenomenon of history. It was as if the historical community, the *milla*, acquired all attributes of faith (*din*). One could even construe it as the coming of modernity through the secularization of Muslim consciousness[9]. A similar shift in the meaning of the term 'scripture' is noticeable in western history. Smith construes this development as a sign of 'detranscendentalization', a

---

7   Smith, Wilfred Cantwell: *Modern Islam in India,* Lahore, 1943, and its better-known sequel, *Islam in Modern History,* Princeton, 1957. His later writings also include: *On Understanding Islam.* The Hague, 1981.

8   Cf: *The Meaning and End of Religion.* New York, 1962; *Towards a World Theology: faith and the comparative history of religion.* London, 1981; also, *Faith and Belief.* New York, 1979.

9   *The Meaning and End. Op. cit.* pp.88-118.

move away from value-laden theological consciousness to a putatively value-free sociological one[10].

The fateful dichotomy of religion and secularity, upon which most of modernity's self-authentication hinges, is an ideological claim rather than a 'scientific' theory. At any rate, it has received the critical gaze of a Muslim scholar, Talal Asad, who unfortunately does not figure at all in Alatas's paper[11]. In his seminal work *Genealogy of Religion,* Asad sought to uncover the genealogy of the modern concept. His effort resulted in the discovery of 'religion' as a secular construct. He also argued against the anthropologists' attempts to give 'religion' a generic definition, because 'not only its constituent elements and relationships are historically specific, but because that definition is itself the historical product of discursive forces.' The modern search for the essence of 'religion', he warned, invites one to separate it conceptually from the domain of power. It may be, Asad observes wryly, 'a happy accident that this effort of defining religion converges with the liberal demand in our times that it be kept quite separate from politics, law and science - spaces in which varieties of power and reason articulate our distinctive modern life. This definition is at once part of a strategy (for secular liberals) of the confinement, and (for liberal Christians) of the defence of religion.'

The liberal theory of the separation of religion from power, Asad also asserts, brings no epistemological dividends when it comes to the understanding of Islam. For, to insist that politics and religion - two distinct

---

10   *What is Scripture.* London, SCM press, 1993. Cf. our review: 'TRANSCENDENCE AND TEX-TUALITY: Deconstructing the authorship of the reader', in *MWBR,* 14:4, summer 1994, pp.3-8).
11   Cf: Talal Asad: *The Idea of an Angthropology of Islam.* Center for Contemporary Arab Stud-ies, Georgetown University, Washington, 1986; also, *Genealogies of Religion: Discipline and Rea-sons of Power in Christianity and Islam.* The Johns Hopkins University Press, Baltimore. 1993, and *Formation of the Secular: Christianity, Islam, Modernity.* Stanford University Press, 2003. A recent study that presents Asad's contribution to the modern discourse on secularism and enters into a critical dialogue with his thought is: *Powers of the Secular Modern: Talal Asad and His Interlocutors.* Ed. By David Scott & Charles Hirschkind. Standord University Press, 2006.

essences that modern society succeeds in segregating both conceptually and practically - have been coupled in the Muslim tradition, he argued, is 'to take up an a priori position in which religious discourse in the political arena is seen as a disguise for political power.' Or, viewed differently, Asad suggests that in order to achieve self-realization, a historically specific Islam is not obliged to severe itself from the existing sources of power[12]. In sum, Asad's genealogy of the anthropological idea of religion as 'a particular history of knowledge and power out of which the modern world has been constructed' is a masterly feat of penetrating scholarship. Or, expressed more candidly: "Religion" is the foundational myth of secularism.

Sociology as the Handmaiden of Modernity

The word 'social' is Latin in origin and has no equivalent in Greek language. Instead, there exists from earliest times, a 'con-fusion' between the two. Seneca, for instance, translates the Aristotelian *zoon politikon* by *animal socialis*. Apparently, the Latin usage of the word *societas* originally had a distinguishable, albeit limited, political signification. The equation between the political and the social realms has acquired added ambiguities in the modern discourse. According to Hannah Arendt:

'The distinction between a private and a public sphere of life corresponds to the household and the political realm, which have existed as distinct, separate entities at least since the rise of the ancient city-state; but the emergence of the social realm which is neither private nor public, strictly speaking, is a relatively new phenomenon whose origin coincided with the emergence of the modern age and which found its political form in the nation-state.'[13]

---

12   Cf. our review of Asad's *Genealogies of Religion* in *Journal of Islamic Studies*, Oxford University press, vol. 6, no. 1 (January 1995), pp. 142-4.

13   Arendt, Hannah: *The Human Condition.* The University of Chicago Press, Chicago & London, 1958. P. 58.

One could say, a bit provocatively, that social science is modernity's counterpart of, and its epistemological antidote to, religion. Sociology sees its mission as the abolition (*Aufhegung*) of the religious modes of articulation of a human reality that is perceived historical through and through![14] What distinguishes modern man from his predecessors is the discovery of 'society'. Or, as expressed by a modern critic: "While Greek man came into contact with and came to know his nature through the political regime of the city, it is by means of society that modern man comes in contact with and comes to know his new element, history. Contemporary society is history that has become the route that is followed, the truth that is accepted, and life that is shared".[15] In other words, the term 'society', which is elaborated through the umpteenth discourses of sociology, is more than a descriptive term or a neutral conceptual tool with universal applicability. It is designed to proclaim the uniqueness of modern western polities and separate them from what came before or what exists today in an outdated form. Far from being universal, then, the worldview of sociology is elitist, reinforcing the claim of Western supremacy as a structural fact of history. (It is not accidental that despite their identical conceptual schemata and methodological assumptions, *sociology* is the science of the civilized, *anthropology* that of the primitives.) Weber, whose sociology incorporates a model of development and an evolutionary historical scheme, may therefore be crowned as the ideologue of the West: 'Weber transmuted the rift between a European past and present into one between the West and the Rest and succeeded along the way in casting out the Rest from the history as completely as Hegel had before him'.[16]

---

14   Cf. for instance: Gauchet, Marcel: *The Disenchantment of the World: A Political History of Religion*. Princeton University Press, 1997 (1985).

15   Pierre Manent: *The City of Man*. Princeton University Press, 998. P. 50.

16   Harootunian, Harry: *The Empire's New Clothes: Paradigm Lost and Regained*. Prickly Paradigm Press, Chicago, 2004. P. 48.

There are other traits of sociological disciplines worth noting. Social science was institutionalized only late in the nineteenth century and it emerged under the shadow of natural science, i.e. Newtonian physics. According to a modern theoretician, 'Social science was like someone tied to two horses galloping in opposite directions.'[17] It internalized the struggle between Nature and Culture – natural science and humanities – that was characteristic of the clash between epistemological approaches (*Methodenstreit*). Three disciplines were created to deal with the modern world: political science, economic and sociology. What is significant in these attempts to create a systematic structure of modern knowledge is the fact that this epistemological scheme directly corresponds to the perceived hierarchy of cultures and civilizations. According to Wallerstein, these disciplinary subdivisions reflected three underlying cleavages: 'the split between past (history) and present (economics, political science and sociology); the split between the Western civilized world (the above four disciplines) and the rest of the world (anthropology for "primitive" peoples and Oriental studies for non-Western "high civilizations"); and the split, valid only for the modern Western world between the logic of the market (economics), the state (political science), and civil society (sociology).'[18]

The sociological vision with its deterministic outlook, its adoption of the perspective of the spectator rather than that of the agent, its devaluation of politics by separating state from society, its teleological orientation, which in Marxist theory is expressed by the Messianic hope of the disappearance of the state altogether, and a host other myths about the end of history and so on, make it less distinguishable from metaphysics than it cares to acknowledge. Even the nature of the sociological causality

17   Wallerstein, Immanuel: *The Uncertainties of Knowledge*. Temple University Press, Philadelphia, 2004. P. 19.
18   *Ibid.*

is problematic from a humanistic point of view. In fact, sociology achieves its 'scientific' status by ignoring the problem of Man altogether; by bartering his subjectivity (moral freedom) for an objectivity that leaves out the most essential traits of his humanity, the transcendent dimension as it were. This fact is expressed perceptively by a contemporary philosopher as such: "As soon as the humanity of man is posited as a cause, another viewpoint than the causal viewpoint is taken on the human world, one which sees man as an agent confronting the uncertainty of the future...... On the other hand, if one considers man as an effect, then everything is different. There is no longer any real uncertainty, only a scientific difficulty.'[19]

From the Islamic point of view, sociology's teleological Eurocentrism is a venial sin; its mutilated, detranscendentalized image of Man is far more grievous. Islamic consciousness would also hold that any sociological representation of the human reality, including that of Muslim history and civilization, is the gift of a reductionist epistemology that achieves its object, the construction of sociological facts, by leaving out that which is essentially and ineluctably human. The same applies to other modes of self-authentication in modernity, its political and ideological discourses. Modern man is able to sustain his imperialist vision by eschewing a politics of humanity. Muslim self-awareness, however, generates critical perspectives on the givens of the modernist discourse and its supremacist pretensions. The cultivation of such a critical consciousness is indispensable to the dispelling of the intellectual haze that is the gift of the Islamophobic imagination. Hopefully, this symposium will help us bring some clarity to the theme of conceptual chaos and find some remedies for it.

---

19   Manent, P. *op. cit.* p 60.

Islamic Politics or Politics of Islam?*

Amr G.E. Sabet (Schweden)

The process of understanding and conceptualizing the relationship between Islamic Politics and Politics of Islam is one of complexity and subtlety as well as of risk and intrigue. It is complex and subtle because in many cases the two are organically linked and intertwined. Islamic politics by necessity if not by definition incorporates politics of Islam. Risk and intrigue however, emanate from the fact that the opposite does not necessarily hold true. Politics of Islam does not inevitably reflect Islamic politics. Mixing them both is a major source of confusion, uncertainty and disorientation. In many ways, the problem is similar to mystification of ontology and epistemology on the methodological level, strategy and tactics in political and military decision-making, constant values and changing circumstances or conditions on the level of parameters and variables, and consistency and discrepancy at the operational level. While all may be organically linked, inherent in their relationships however, are potential contradictions. When epistemology, for instance, continually falls back on its ontology, dialectically or otherwise, this is a case for a consistent *self-referential* method of thinking. In the different case where epistemology refers to an alien ontology, such as when, for example, Islamic values are justified in terms of an external knowledge system, the outcome is very different and likely

* Original material published in Islam and the Political: Theory, Governance and International Relations © Amr G E Sabet 2008, Pluto Press, London

to be *other-referential*. The same holds true when we talk about strategy and tactics. The best of strategies could be supported or undermined by consistent or discrepant tactics respectively. By the same line of reasoning, politics of Islam may consolidate Islamic politics, or in some cases may go so far so as to undermine it. Involved of course are issues of methodological performance, but also of credibility in the light of which micro politics i.e. the details, the trees, are tested against the macro politics i.e. the broad picture, the forest. This requires creative and mutually buttressing *theoretical* conceptualization and understanding competencies and capabilities.

Theories, as Kenneth Waltz has observed, are made "creatively" (Waltz 1979:9). "The paradox of creativity is that it requires both great familiarity with a subject matter, *and* the ability to approach it from a fresh angle" (Kleindorfer, Kunreuther & Schoemaker 1993:55). By the same token, it must follow a "due process of inquiry" which relates the logic, procedures, and choice of appropriate approaches, to the relevant subject matter (Landau 1972: 219–221; quoted by Waltz 1979:13). The process of creativity is, thus, strongly correlated with the problematization of issues and the search for alternatives; in Islamic parlance, with *genuine ijtihad*. Limitations caused by self–imposed constraints, connected to feelings of "self–discouragement" that a particular course of theoretical creativity or action policy is not possible, will not work, or cannot be done (Kleindorfer et. al. 1993:55), are in many instances both constituted by and constitutive of ideological perceptions. An interrelated system of preferences is at play which connects intellectual creativity to ideology. A relationship is particularly tenuous when a religious worldview limits the horizons of preferences or adaptations that can be made with respect to an opposing worldview or an order, domestic or global, not of its own making.

To theorize is at the same time to conceptualize, and to conceptualize is to understand. "'Understanding' ... means ... having whatever ideas and concepts are needed to recognize that a great many different phenomena are part of a coherent whole" (Heisenberg 1971:33). While a total agreement on the truth–value of subsumed propositions or assumptions may remain wanting, a frame of reference nevertheless exists which informs an intellectual structure of developed themes. This involves a series of processes by which theoretical matrices achieve a significant measure of relative *consensus* and comprehension in any particular community. Conceptualization, in other words, allows for undergoing the theoretical process by which advancement, from the level of abstract ideas or constructs toward policy development and application, can be made. It guards against confusion and *ad hoc* decision– making, and serves to set and sustain subsequent policies within a coherent strategic framework. It follows, therefore, that a lack of conception or of a conceptual reference entails a lack of and inability to understand or comprehend. It further means that the ability to tackle the flow of information becomes acutely diminished, and so is the capacity to judge or make decisions of strategic nature. Failing to conceptualize and/or process information preempts the competence to act.

Conceptualization and intellectual sophistication are necessary conditions for understanding and action, yet their effectiveness lie essentially in the ability of ideas and beliefs to create or construct a corresponding reality. Mental structures or imagery may or may not correspond to objective material conditions. They cannot be assumed as intertwined or directly correlated. Where self–conception or identity *dialectically* coincides with structural reality, satisfaction may ensue and the *status quo* safeguarded. Where this is not the case, and wide discrepancy exists between the two constitutive dimensions, a sense of crisis develops which is detrimental to a culture or a civilization's strength of character, equanimity and consistency. This makes the issue of identity, or "what makes *us* believe we are the same and *them* different ... inseparable from security" (Booth 1997:6), and this is essentially a political issue.

Islam in contemporary times has been facing real and serious challenges to its identity structure from a rapidly transforming world and a concomitantly changing order of values. The resulting imbalances and confusion that inflicted Muslims in effectively all their social, political, economic, strategic, and religious domains, have imposed on them soul searching questions of existential significance, about *what has gone wrong and, what is to be done*. These questions have been wrestled with by many Muslims, scholars as well as laymen, in their different ways, largely since the 19th century till current times. Yet no clear consensus has been reached or unambiguous answers have been finalized. These seemingly perennial questions continue to impose themselves, calling for additional efforts which can help in systematizing a way of thinking that has so far remained too incoherent, apologetic, and abstract. This way of thinking was problematic in the fashion it sought to link social theory with Islamic thought, or in its attempt to tackle modern as well as post–modern concerns from a supposedly Islamic perspective. It has not been uncommon for example — depending on circumstances, background, or predispositions — that socialist or liberal–democratic ideas be re–packaged as basically Islamic principles: it was Islam which had always called for social justice, and it was Islam which had always upheld democracy and freedom. Much in this work attempts to challenge and contest such defensive and apologetic approaches. Mechanisms in general, are intertwined with the values upholding them, and democracy whether it be a concept or a sheer procedure cannot be separated from its liberal, and therefore, secular umbilical cord. It becomes a high point of politics therefore to illustrate how and why Islamic values, principles of governance, and global relations must be differentiated from those of liberal and democratic notions, if they are to remain as *necessary* parameters, not merely as contingent variables. "The high points of politics" as Carl Schmitt has put it, "are simultaneously the moments in which the enemy is, in concrete clarity, recognized as the enemy" (Schmitt 1976: 67). By enemy here is not necessarily meant a sole relationship of hostility but as significantly, of *demarcation*. This calls for questioning Western concepts, which have come to occupy a position of 'Truth'. It calls also for emphasizing the need to rethink narratives of triumphant secularism and its liberal assumptions about what is politically and morally essential to modern life. This is a prerequisite for expanding Islamic theoretical frameworks, to revitalize Islamic thought and to suggest possible alternatives, using analytical and empirical tools. For the main faults of Islamic classical thought as well as some contemporary views informed by it, as Abdul–Hamid Abu–Sulayman has observed, are located not in content but in methodology. Those faults were linked to the absence of a clear conceptualization of the space–time dimension, lack of empiricism (with the notable exception of Ibn Khaldun), and of a rigorous systematic approach to the development of Islamic social and human sciences (Sulayman 1993:87–94).

I wish to stress, however, that it is not the purpose here to attempt to make any claims toward some form of 'Islamization of knowledge' or for that matter, its secularization — claims which I believe harbor more problems than they resolve. Rather the aim is toward the *integration* of knowledge, secular or religious. This attempt at integrating Islamic thought and social theory should be done with the purpose of linking objectives of *decolonization* at all human levels in order to underscore Islam's liberating commitment not only toward Muslims, but toward humanity at large. The decolonization process that had taken place during the Post WW II era remains, unfortunately, an unfinished, and even a regressing project. It could no longer be simply reduced to nominal political independence of the colonized when, in fact, colonialism is well and thriving, with a good dose of domestic counterpart added to it. In addition to the political, as well as the economic, there is the essential need for independence of thought, and from thereon, the mental, psychological, and the spiritual; in essence that is, exorcising a soul that has been possessed and liberating a mind that has been colonized. While 'exorcising' may constitute the most difficult and tormenting phase of decolonization, it is at this level nevertheless that the ambiguities and ambivalences of incomplete and partial forms of decolonization must be addressed. This can be performed through the development of an anti–imperialist multicultural reformation process of knowledge, of polities, economies and societies, which Islam is eminently qualified to support and sustain. Exorcising, therefore, necessitates never losing sight of preserving and maintaining independence of the ontological and epistemological foundations of Islam, as well as its spirit and universality. It perhaps also involves an acknowledgment that it may still be too early to talk about a 'post–colonial' phase.

On the Internal Condition of the Muslim World

At this historical juncture, much of the Muslim world appears to be in a state of disarray. There appears to be no clear vision as to where it stands, what determining role its faith should play, and what, as a community of God (*umma*) is the horizon of its action and position among nations. As a matter of faith, Muslims believe they are entitled to a leading position, not simply as a role but as a mission and obligation (Qur'an 2:143; 22:78; 48:28). Evading such responsibilities carries its own penalties, both worldly and beyond.[1] As far

---

1 For instance: "Thus, have We made of you an Umma justly balanced, that ye might be witnesses over the nations, and the Messenger a witness over yourselves (Qur'an 2:143; www. IslamiCity.com).

as this world is concerned, strategically speaking, "[e]ligible states [and nations] that fail to attain great power status are predictably punished" (Layne 1995:134). This maxim is made as a matter of starting point. Yet other consequences follow — political, military, social, and economic — all merging into the crucible of cultural domination and identity formation. The first step of persuading the Muslim community to undercut its own eligibility, is followed by means and methods aiming at throwing it back on the defensive, leveling accusations against it such as 'fundamentalism,' 'terrorism,' 'extremism,' among a range of other possibilities. The idea is to make an opponent or adversary, in this case the Muslims, "uneasy and apologetic" about any objective or objectives it may have or wish to pursue. This would constitute "a first small step in the process of those objectives' *"erosion"* inducing a dynamic through which the 'adversary' would start discarding them (Harkabi 1977:88).[2] This then allows for a continuous process of chipping away at the *will* and resistance of the antagonist, creating new space for the hegemonic induction of new ideas and identity altering structures associated with claims of superiority and universality. As former US national security advisor Zbigniew Brzezinski pointed out, "cultural superiority, successfully asserted and quietly conceded," has the effect of "reducing the need to rely on large military forces to maintain the power of the imperial center" (Brzezinski 1997:21). The purpose is to generate a good degree of compliance among members of a targeted group, as "the successful state, like the successful criminal, wishes to enjoy [the] spoils in peace and this requires a measure of consent ... from the victims ..." (Reynolds 1989:5).

Such dynamics call for an engaging ability to observe, to conceptualize, to understand, and to theorize, as a prerequisite, most importantly, to planning, organizing,

---

2   Yehoshafat Harkabi was a former Chief of Israeli Military intelligence (1955-1959), and an advisor on intelligence to former Israeli Prime Minister Menachem Begin.

and acting. This is a protracted, risky and arduous *process*. Yet as challenging as it may be, it has been facilitated by the fact that a religio–historical experience, represented by the Iranian Islamic revolution, is actually unfolding on the global landscape in the realm of *praxis*. The dialectics of theory and praxis may thus be 'at hand.' Such *dialectics* propose the Iranian Islamic revolutionary experience as a model to be studied and evaluated based largely on self–referential Islamic standards. Secondly, they link and embed this experience's unfolding religious, theoretical, and practical manifestations into the dynamics of Islamic history. This is a means of contributing to a possible intellectual reorientation in the field of social theory, as well as in that of *madhabi* or Islamic paradigmatic communities. Thirdly, they help identify certain process and structural distinctions between what case actually constitutes an Islamic system or regime exercising Islamic politics, as opposed to one that makes claims to be one, simply instrumentalizing politics of Islam.

A brief comparison of approaches to the nature of systems in the two countries of Iran and Saudi Arabia may help underscore the significance of dialectical distinctions, and provide justifications for theoretical and/or empirical choices made in this study. Both countries harbor systems which present themselves as Islamic.[3] Consequently, Lawrence Davidson (1998) set both Iran and Saudi Arabia in a common Islamic "fundamentalist" framework. In many ways, this is problematic and disinforming. Structurally speaking, Saudi Arabia is a feudal dynastic and absolute monarchy ruling by the right of conquest, (Nehme 1998:278, 286 & 287). It bears much of the negative characteristics of the historical Umayyad dynasty (680–750 AD), whose founding ruling figures continue to occupy a seminal position in Wahhabism, the Saudi pseudo cult. Ibn Taymiyya (1263–1328 AD), its precursor, was a staunch sympathizer

---

3   Parts of the following analysis have been borrowed from Sabet (2000).

of the corrupt and transgressing (*bughat*) Umayyads, at times even against the house of the Prophet (*Al al–Bayt*). The Umayyad dynasty also, was considered to be the 'Sunni' state par excellence, as opposed to its Shi'i opposition and enemy. Yet, it was never perceived as 'fundamentalist.' Furthermore, the Umayyad state is acknowledged, in significantly large and influential Muslim quarters, to have brought about the historical shift, away from Islamic Caliphate (*Khilafa*) to the corrupt form of tyrannical and hereditary kingship (*al–mulk al–adud*). If the Saudi–Umayyad analogy stands, then one may conclude that Saudi Arabia, notwithstanding its extensive ritualistic trappings, is neither 'fundamentalist' nor Islamic, whether structurally or in the basic thrust of its policies and attitudes (process).[4] In terms of structure, it is '*mulk adud.*' In terms of process, as Naveed Shaikh has perceptively observed, "division [of Arabs and Muslims] rather than unification, had always been the preferred way" of the Saudi regime "to maintain leverage" (Shaikh 2003:34). With American help, this regime's perpetual policy of opposing the rise of any Arab or Islamic regional power — be it Egypt, during President Gamal abdel Nasser's time (1954–1970), or current Islamic Iran — essentially served to render Israel the real and sole regional power. This policy orientation constituted the real foundation of the *de facto* complicity between Israel and the Saudi regime. An anachronistic feudal hypocrisy is then equated with the Iranian Islamic regime, a system based on the principal structural components of *allegiance* (*baya'a*/stem = Wilayat al– faqih) and *choice* (*ikhtiar*/branch = presidency), and whose general religio–political thrust is legitimate in terms of its independence, self–reliance, credible respect and preservation of Islamic dignity and values internally and *vis–à–vis* the external world.

---

4   One of course has to distinguish here between being a Muslim society and, being Islamic in the sense that the structure and process of the state coincide and are congruent with the totality of Islamic values rather than its appearances, that is, *ritualism.*

If this assessment stands, then why is Iran designated as, 'fundamentalist' and not just as Islamic?[5] What purpose does a 'fundamentalist' qualification serve? More importantly, what justification is there in the first place to include both regimes in a common framework? This raises serious questions about the viability of studies, which adopt such undistinguishing approaches. By attributing an Islamic character to both regimes where one of which is not Islamic, and a 'fundamentalist' label to both when neither is, one can imagine the amount and extent of confusion that such a framework of conflicting logics may generate. It would provide an opportunity for what may be termed *intellectual strategic deception*. The whole idea behind such deception is to get an opposite party to confuse its purpose and understanding, and/or to do what one wants, consciously, or, better still, unconsciously. Essentially that is, to get an opponent to lose his/her sense of conception. This would serve two main purposes. First, by subtly and deceptively equating an Islamic regime with a non–Islamic one it creates confusion — throwing the needle into the haystack so to speak. Second, it *liberates* any presumably hostile policy toward Islam, separating religious from political targeting theoretically, while targeting both practically. Consequently, Davidson, for instance, can make the claim that American hostility to one 'variant' of Islamic interpretation is not to be perceived as targeting Islam but only policy behavior, or merely an 'interpretation.' American–Saudi 'friendly' relations are then introduced as an alibi and a confirmation (Davidson 1998:xiii–xiv). King Abdullah of Saudi Arabia, for instance, at one point of time built–up by American media as a "Saudi Desert Fox" who sought to "take the lead in a strife–torn Middle East," 'brushing aside' the United States. This polishing–up process sounded eerily similar to the one in the early 1980s when, shortly before attacking Iran, Saddam Hussain was hailed by the same media as 'Bismarck of the

---

5 It should be pointed out that this term has by now increasingly fallen out of usage.

Arabs.' In case there are any doubts, *Newsweek* Magazine for instance sought to remind the King of Plato's saying: "He who refuses to rule is liable to be ruled by one worse than himself [read Iran]" (Newsweek 9 April 2007:20–21). The underlying message or subtle threat sounded like, either you lead against Iran, or Iran would lead instead. No wonder that at the Riyadh 19th Arab Summit held on 28–29 March 2007, the King ironically adopted Arab nationalist jargon, so unbefitting of Saudi Arabia. In addition, the conference's final statement, the "Riyadh Declaration," reiterated peace with Israel to be a "strategic choice" — a choice that seems to be reasserted every time some form of aggression against an Arab or Islamic country is in the offing. This is a clear case of the negative and undermining aspects that may be termed 'the politics of Islam' as opposed to *Islamic politics*. The latter is transformed into a divergent exogenous thrust rather than a consistent endogenous form of consolidation.

Some Muslim intellectuals, therefore, including prominent figures such as Hasan al–Banna and Sayyed Qutb, tended to step into murky waters when they claimed that as long as the *Shari'ah* (Islamic Law) is implemented, an Islamic regime could take any form. While there is always room for *differentiation*, this is very different from open-ended statements of the kind. The actual and *bona fide* application of the Shari'ah, as a matter of fact, would prohibit this. Moreover, notwithstanding variations, there must be some predominantly common features and idiosyncrasies so that a regime may be defined as Islamic or, more significantly, as non–Islamic even if it alleges to apply the Shari'ah or its pretenses. This is a most important intellectual challenge, which demands the setting of parameters and constraints on the instrumental manipulation of religion (politics of Islam). Precise standards of religio–intellectual *falsification* and *affirmation* are required in order to avoid capricious and uninformed judgments. After all Saudi Arabia claims to 'apply' the Shari'ah. Would not this therefore, justify a monarchic hereditary system as well as its policies? From where they know or do not know, some Islamists have provided the intellectual cover for such discrepancies.

Perhaps a different conceptual perspective which may allow us to better identify or define what constitutes Islamic politics relates to the concept of assabiyya (core or nucleus solidarity) or assabiyyat al-Islam, as an inherently religio-political concept. As a *religious* concept it incorporates the Shari'ah, as a *political* concept it incorporates distinctions, dichotomies, and boundaries. In the latter lay the essence of Arab and Muslims dilemmas. Divested of *will* and unable to determine their own friend or enemy, a variant of self and other, existing Arab regimes have relinquished their political existence to external powers; a condition of total loss of assabiyya. This is so because it would be a mistake to believe, as Carl Schmitt has put it, that a nation could eliminate the distinction of friend and enemy by declaring its friendship for the entire world or by voluntarily disarming itself. The world will not thereby become depoliticized, and it will not be transplanted into a condition of pure morality, pure justice, or pure economics. If a people is afraid of the trials and risks implied by existing in the sphere of politics, then another people will appear which will assume these trials by protecting it against foreign enemies and thereby taking over political rule. The protector then decides who the enemy is by virtue of the eternal relation of protection and obedience (Schmitt 1976: 51 –52).

The overtaking power, the US in this case, stepped in to define for these regimes their own people and their own faith, as well as Islamic Iran, as the enemy, introducing Israel in the process as a friend. Consequently, a new geo-strategic and political system continues to evolve in the abode of Islam in the image of the *enemy*. Its stalwart pillars include (neo)liberal democratic discursive conceptualizations strongly intertwined with mechanisms of socio and geo-political fragmentation and structures of economic and military intimidation. This package of discourse, mechanisms and policies, has come to serve the geo-strategic purposes of negatively evolving politics of Islam, practiced by Muslim and non-Muslim States alike. One may recall the politics of Islam during the Cold War. In the same fashion that Islam was hijacked by the US during the Cold War, through Muslim client regimes, for its own benefit, it is now being hijacked again for the same purpose, although in a perverse sense. Instead of fighting America's wars as its fodder, it is now becoming its launching-pad, in all cases its instrumental means. The parallel collapse of Arab competency has significantly facilitated such foreign intrusions and minimized opposition capabilities of regional actors. The American-Israeli alliance which seeks to capitalize and manipulate these new opportunities, matched by a disorganized, fragmentary and uncomprehending Arab regional bewilderment, and a conspicuous panicky collapse of political will, has set the politics of Islam against Islamic politics. Yet, ... as long as a people exists in the political sphere this people must, even if only in the most extreme case ... determine by itself the distinction of friend and enemy. Therein resides the essence of its [religio]–political existence. When it no longer possesses the capacity or the will to make this distinction, it ceases to exist politically [and religiously]. If it permits this decision to be made by another, then it is no longer a politically free people and is absorbed into another political system (Schmitt 1976: 49).

Once absorbed, it ceases to be Islamic politics despite any fidelity claims to the Shari'ah and transforms into merely being politics of Islam. Thus, Ayatollah Khomeini's depiction of the United States as the "Great Satan" far from simply being a hostile characterization of that country, cuts through this maze of confusion and sets the boundaries of determination. In as far as it identifies the friend/enemy grouping in an Islamic image and establishes an autonomous focus of legitimacy it constitutes a high point of Islamic politics which rearms, focuses, mobilizes and frees. In this sense it is possible to claim that assabiyyat al-Islam resides today in the *'Persians.'* This has much less to do with labels of moderation or extremism as with a clear understanding and conceptualization of both politics and Islam. Such an understanding helps in the linking of Abd al–Rahman Ibn Khaldun's (1332–1406 AD) concept of *assabiyya* with the principle of *Wilayat al–Faqih* in a potentially well-developed conceptual and theoretical as well as praxis framework. This is the case even if some ambiguities have been associated with the use of assabiyya that call for additional clarifications regarding its designation as an Islamic concept.

Ibn Khaldun's notion of *assabiyya* has been largely understood and judged by contemporary scholars in the very terms that the great historian had used, over six centuries ago, to refer to tribal solidarities. No serious attempts have been made to expand it or to re–infuse the concept so as to render it more relevant to contemporary forms of solidarities, linking it for instance to socio–political theories of hegemony (a la Gramsci), elites (Perato, Mosca, Michels), vanguards (Lenin), or Wilayat al–Faqih (Ayatollah Khomeini), among other possibilities. Furthermore, claims that the Khaldunian concept, approach and methodology were *Islamic* are further met with skepticism, as not particularly linked to the ways of 'real' Islamic thought, and as being closer instead to the presumably 'universal' aspects of social theory. Reconstructing the concept of assabiyya would allow for its extension, beyond conventional and narrow, possibly tribal Khaldunian connotations, in order to apply it to contemporary structures and contingencies. This requires further exposition.

First and at the outset, as one of the two pillars of a possible theory and principle of hegemonic leadership it is significant to note that assabiyya comes from the root Arabic word 'ASB which means the nerve or the command center of something. It refers, that is, to the ability to exercise *will* power, the foundation of any genuine Islamic politics. To say for instance, that Arab will has collapsed, at least at the regimes level, or that they are incapable of exercising it, is to say they cannot by definition practice such politics and that therefore, the assabiyya of Islam cannot be invested in them. This means they are neither politically nor Islamically viable. More recently, a Turkish 'model' under the Justice and Development Party (AKP) has been introduced as an 'enlightened' alternative of Islamic politics. This is so even though Turkey as a model is at best simply instrumentalizing and practicing a form of politics of Islam. The real threat to Islamic politics is that Turkey has been pushed to perform the same manipulative role that countries like Saudi Arabia and Pakistan played during the Cold War against the Communist bloc and the forces of Arab Nationalism, but this time against Islam. The idea would be to present it as an alternative and rival model of the Iranian experience – an American Islam or politics of Islam in a new guise so to speak. As a matter of fact, as far back as 1998, the *Economist* suggested such a strategy to be pursued toward Turkey. It described that country as NATO's "front line" state against the spread of Islamic fundamentalism, to be fashioned as the model of a "moderate secular" Muslim state and "an example of how it is possible to be Muslim and democratic at the same time" (*Economist*, 1 August 1998: 14). By way of strategic deception, Arab, American and Turkish politics of Islam is to be confused with Islamic politics in order to confound the reality of the situation away from where the assabiyya of Islam (Wilayat al-Faqih) should be invested and recognized.

The AKP and Turkey, therefore, face three main options and challenges. If the AKP performance on the one hand were to eventually crystallize into a form of genuine Islamic politics, the risk factor and external as well as internal pressures will multiply and all the contradictions which it had sought to resolve between secularism, liberalism and democracy on one hand, and Islam on the other will most likely burst out into the open. The country will be in for a rough ride. If, on the other hand, it simply chooses to practice Islamic politics within the context of the strategy suggested by the *Economist*, it is likely to become just another Islamic façade rather than a model of any kind. As a matter of fact, the first and major challenge that the AKP will have to face to begin to establish its genuine Islamic credentials is to undermine and demolish external hegemonic and penetrating infrastructures in the country. This is a foremost prerequisite, for if Turkey is to institute itself as an Islamic model, it has to acquire a credible assabiyya. Something no superimposed Western value system, even if disguised in the form of politics of Islam, can provide. If, in contradistinction, one may take the proclamations by AKP officials that their party is committed to the secular values of the Turkish State at face value, then the AKP may turn out to be something akin to the Christian Democratic parties of Europe. It may simply be a reflection of a new, perhaps an evolving case of a secular liberal democratic system which may attempt to moderate the radical secularism of post-Ottoman Turkey, but essentially is a continuation of its path. That is, more of the same. In this case any talk about Islamic politics, politics of Islam, or assabiyya become largely irrelevant. In the face of such choices all the political skills that had served to bring the AKP to power may turn out to have been the easy part.

Second, there has been rather negative religious connotations associated with the concept of assabiyya as a reflection of chauvinism and/or nepotism — characteristics Prophet Muhammad is reported to have condemned. It is reported that he had said, regarding assabiyya, "forsake it for it is rotten" (author's translation). Imam Ali, the Prophet's cousin and son in law, when asked whether loving one's own kinfolk constituted assabiyya, elaborated that the assabiyya that was condemned was that by which one perceives the wicked of one's own (kinfolk, tribe or group, nation) to be better than the virtuous of others. What we have here of course are religio–moral statements. They are about a particular form that assabiyya might take as a potential source of prejudice and injustice, or as a cause of action or attitude not constrained or subsumed under an Islamic hierarchy of meaning or sanction.

The positive significance of the consolidating and organizational aspects of assabiyya however, has never been lost to early Muslims. Despite Islam's call for transcending structures and affiliations based on such an organizing principle, this was meant in a *reductive* rather than in a *negating* sense. When early Muslim armies prepared to engage in battle, they sought to *capitalize* on such feelings of assabiyya by positioning members of same tribes together, rather than diffusing them as individuals in the mass of the Islamic army. This had been the case long before Ibn Khaldun developed his theory, and who as a Muslim historian must have been well aware of. His usage of the concept, therefore, does not refer to its negative aspects but to the general sentiments of solidarity, which bring people together in order to create society, the foundation of any eventual good. Assabiyya in this sense signifies not only those primordial feelings, which are embedded in the natural ties of kinship and blood relations, but also to the broader context of group cohesion, affiliation and common concerns — an *esprit de corps* of sorts. It embodies the moral, natural and functional purposes of human social and political existence organized around those who lead and those who are led. While Ibn Khaldun stresses the concept in its 'sociological' aspect, and is thus perceived to be making some 'truth' statements/assumptions about human nature, this does not deprive assabiyya of its Islamic character but rather *affirms* it. Islamic concepts incorporate the universal and the relative, the abstract and the concrete.

Ibn Khaldun simply adopted assabiyya in its reductive form informed by Islamic history and conditions. After all, if knowledge is perceived as socially constructed, or society to be constructed by "knowledgeable practices" (Wendt 1992:392), in either or both cases, Ibn Khaldun has been the product of Islamic society and Islamic knowledge. His conceptual framework therefore, remains *embedded* and *grounded*. Even as he attempted to identify the historical causes behind the rise and fall of nations or civilizations, he did not isolate such developments from God's design and unfolding plan. Ibn Khaldun made it clear that God's will, as *primary* cause pertaining to the rise or fall of a nation, a ruling dynasty, or a regime, worked through the *secondary* cause of an opposing assabiyya; a feeling or a condition which God bestows, in His mercy and wisdom, and as a matter of will on a selected or chosen people, in and for a specified time. In other words, Ibn Khaldun did not separate the sociological aspects of assabiyya from the unfolding Divine laws or *sunnan* of *circulation* (*tadawul*= rise and fall of nations at the *reduced* social theory level), *substitution* (*istibdal/haymanah*=substitution/domination or hegemony, at the *reduced* social theory level) of nations, and/or *checking* one nation against another (*tadafu'*= action–reaction, stimulus–response, or balance of power at the *reduced* social theory level).[6] His effort constitutes the foundational meaning of an Islamic philosophy of history and empowerment which, by including God "among the dramatis personae of history gives history itself a new dimension" (Toynbee 1972:492).

Such a hierarchy of meaning is inherent in Ibn Khaldun's approach. He in fact observed that the *assabiyya of Islam* was being invested in the Turks of his time. This was consistent with the Prophetic tradition that had heralded the eventual conquest of Constantinople and

---

6 .... And did not Allah Check one set of people by means of another, the earth would indeed be full of mischief: But Allah is full of bounty to all the worlds (Qur'an 2:251; www.IslamiCity.com).

praised the conquering army and its Prince (although there was no mention of who the people or the Prince might be, this was nevertheless an event that took place at a later date in 1453 AD by an Ottoman army led by Muhammad the Conqueror. The Turks are universally understood to be the referents of this hadith). If, by the same line of reasoning, Prophet Muhammad had heralded the 'resurgence' of Islam at the hands of the Persians sometime in the future, one may *understand* this to be intimation to the endowment of the Persians with assabiyya — an additional 'Islamic' justification for the choice of the Iranian case and its linking with Ibn Khaldun's theory within a common Islamic framework.[7]

On the External Condition of the Muslim World

The above approach proposes a theory of state or governance, based on the concepts of assabiyya, and of Wilayat al–Faqih, and is a prerequisite to a broader Islamic theory of international relations. The conceptual reconstruction and expansion that develops allows for an Islamic approach that connects the internal/domestic and external/international imperatives of religious values, and sets a framework within which Islamic — non–Islamic relations are conducted. By overriding the internal–external separating boundaries of the domestic and the international, the theory of the internal or domestic becomes at the same time a theory of the external — a potentially *global* Islamic alternative.

---

7   The 'Islamic' justification for the choice of Iran and *Wilayat al–Faqih* here as a most relevant leadership principle, is based on the Prophetic Tradition narrated by *Abu– Huraira*, the companion of the Prophet. When the Qur'anic verse "... if ye turn back (from the path), He will substitute in your stead another people [non–Arab?]; then they wouldnot be like you," was revealed (47:39), the Prophet was asked, who those substituting people may be. He put his hand on *Salman al Farisi's* (the only Persian Muslim at the time) shoulder and said "this man and his people. By him in whose hands my soul is, if the faith were to be as far as Pleiades (*al–Thurayya*) [secular epoch?] it shall be brought back by men from Persia [The Islamic Revolution?] (Al–Tabari 1980; v. 26:42). See also Al– Qurtobi (1967; v. 16:258). This does not preclude further rational justifications based on the theory and practice of the Iranian leadership.

Breaking down such boundaries opens the door and justifies the Islamic theory or paradigm of nations even if in a modified fashion. This stands in contrast to and challenges Sulayman's assertion that the classical Islamic theory is no longer relevant and his attempt to *adaptively* "reconstruct" Islamic history in order to fit it into some form of a nation-state framework. Essentially, his approach is not far from others who call for historicizing Islam. Starting from the low threshold that Muslims are intellectually, politically, and technologically weak and backward (Sulayman 1993:61 & 97–98), the thrust of Sulayman's effort pertains to a pragmatic interpretive framework which, sets causal beliefs in conflict with both the Islamic worldview and its principled values. Nowhere is this clearer than when he attempts to justify and explain early Muslim battles with the pagans of Mecca and the Jews, and the rules determining conduct with regard to protected religious minorities (*people of the Book*) (Sulayman 1993:97ff). He stumbles into two main pitfalls. First, he gives precedence to causal factors (i.e. politics of Islam) over the totalizing signification of Islamic events — the cosmological and the principled (i.e. Islamic politics). Instead of being part of a religious history, they are contextualized and historicized. This is not problematic in and of itself provided the hierarchy of meaning is maintained. There may have been immediate reasons behind many of the military and political decisions made by Prophet Muhammad, yet irrespective, they were and always will be embedded in the ordained teleology of Islamic worldview and principled beliefs.

The Arabs had to become Muslims, and only one religion was to be in Arabia.[8] Whether this was achieved peacefully or by war was a contingent matter. The second pitfall, which follows from the first, occurs when Qur'anic

---

8   The Prophet is reported to have said: "I have been commanded to fight until people profess that there is no God but Allah...." The Christians in the southern part of Arabia were also asked by the second Caliph of Islam to choose any place outside of the Arabian Peninsula to inhabit. Though done with full dignity and honor, it was based on the command of the Prophet that there is to be only one religion in Arabia.

verses are also contextualized and thus relativized and historicized, apart from their absolute standards (Sulayman 1993:112). The purpose here is by no means to go through the details of Sulayman's approach or to offer an exhaustive critique, but to show what happens when calls for *historicizing* Islam are heeded. How a historicized approach when cast on the understanding of the Islamic theory of nations, reduces it to a mere ideological framework. Rather than exploring or searching for a possible dialectical link between theory and the modern global condition, Sulayman simply claims that the modern world cannot be explained in terms of the classical concepts and frame of mind (1993:61). Yet, an Islamic social or international theory must always maintain the dialectical relation between the absolute and the relative, otherwise theory even if labeled Islamic, will end up as a reductive secularization of religion. Historicizing that is, reduces and secularizes, and undermines a whole religious and intellectual edifice instead of expanding its horizons.

Several factors nevertheless account for the contemporary strength and continued relevance of this very same classical theory. First, it is embedded in the Islamic worldview, which endows it with both legitimacy and a good measure of longevity if not permanence. While it may have developed over an extended period of time into a theoretical framework, the fact that it is part of the *Shari'ah* and is in principle based on the same sources and maintained by the same sanctions situates it in the overlapping realm of theory and law. It was concerned with external relations as well as with Islamic 'truth.' While the former sets the classical approach in the domain of theory and conception, the latter dimension situates it in the realm of law (Waltz 1979:9), and together in their unity they constitute a paradigm of Islamic politics. This is why the classical framework can be referred to as an Islamic *theory* and as an Islamic *law* of nations interchangeably. While its classical formulation, as an interpretive theory is such that it does not allow for inferences about concrete events and hence may subject it to legitimate critique in this respect (as theory), this is no justification for disposing with it (as law). By consistently incorporating the dimensions of worldview, principled beliefs and causal beliefs the theory *integrates* the subject matter and falls within the domain of what might be termed "*taxonomico– reductive*" theories (Collin 1985: 187). In the field of principled action or praxis, these theories record the "dynamic factors behind action, but without specifying these, or the conditions under which they are activated, in such detail that inferential power ensues" (Collin 1985:187). The Islamic theory's abode of war versus the abode of peace structure simply illustrates two opposing blocs in constant conflict without providing for the possibility of additional inferences, contingencies, or outcomes. Yet its integrative power reigns as the "smallest common denominator between theories which employ the same theoretical vocabulary, but diverge in inferential power." This means that results arrived at for taxonomico– reductive theories are valid for theories of higher inferential power as well (Collin 1985:188) — a strong measure of theoretical consistency. This and the fact that the classical framework integrated both theory and 'law/truth' render it a metatheory — one that theorizes about theories and reinstates Islam as a collective consciousness above that of the modern state. In this sense, it is a "form of preanalysis that disturbs the complacency of received knowledge, its self–evident relations to events, and the 'naturalness' of its language" (Der Derian 1989:7).

Secondly, Islamic theory stands the test of generality and parsimony. It reduces the number of laws and principles needed to account for the data, by replacing a large class of "narrow–scope" principles with a smaller class of more general ones with equal or superior explanatory power (Collin 1985:61). In this Islamic framework, the abode of Islam and the abode of War corresponded to the '*self*' and '*other*' (or the friend/enemy variant) respectively. From thereon developed a whole corpus of scholarly work incorporating narrower principles yet subjecting them to broader autonomous, self–referential constraints. In contrast, Sulayman attempts to present an alternative "dynamic" approach. His is based on the assumptions that decision–makers in Muslim states cannot afford to obey the anachronistic and rigid legal provisions of past ages, and that the value of a foreign policy undertaken by a Muslim state cannot be assessed by traditional legalistic means (Sulayman 1993:147). In a roundabout way, these assumptions start off by constituting a secularized approach to politics, separating foreign policy decision–making from religious underpinnings and constraints. From the outset an ideological position is adopted which magnificently fits the interests of largely illegitimate regimes in the Muslim states, particularly those which seek to project an Islamic façade devoid of substance. His framework basically proposes that any policy devised to address certain circumstances must be decided upon in the light of five conditions. Those ranged from: 1—the basic principles and values of Islam; 2—the character of threats to and the opportunities for the pursuit of Islamic goals; 3—the strengths and limitations of Muslim societies; to 4—the resources of adversaries and allies; and 5—the limitations of the world environment (Sulayman 1993:147). Yet in a seemingly contradictory stance he concludes that, "the nature of policies professed in the Muslim state depends, in the last analysis, on the particular situation at hand" (Sulayman 1993:147). But if such is the case, why is Islam of any significance or importance? It all turns out to be a matter of sheer pragmatism if not outright opportunism, perhaps politics of Islam but certainly not Islamic politics. After all, what if the systemic factors (conditions 4 & 5 above) function in such a way so as not to allow space for Islamic values and principled beliefs?

A crucial issue that Islamic theory must deal with is what is to be done so as to change or influence the global environment in a fashion that would serve Islamic values, the latter being set *a priori*, as the classical theory does. Yet instead of setting Islamic standards (*worldview*) which are to be determined based on principled convictions (*fiqh*), and then pursued through causal beliefs (*fatawa*) (Islamic politics), Sulayman simply takes the global system as a given and then seeks to 'adapt' Islam to it (politics of Islam). While some may agree with such an ordering, the question remains as to why he labels his theoretical focus as 'Islamic,' especially when Muslim structures are constituted rather than constitutive. Sulayman's approach makes a choice of a particular theory of state — that of the modern state. This determined his external international approach. And since the state *unit* as a product of Western history undermines Islamic premises, the systemic whole can only arrive at a 'non– Islamic' conclusion. In adapting to external 'imperatives,' epistemology is inevitably determined by the totally opposing 'ontology' of globalization and systemic inequality, becoming open both to their information and control. Sulayman's pursuit of epistemology (politics of Islam) undermines Islamic ontology (Islamic politics). This is what allows him to conclude that the conditional framework which, he proposes could accommodate every shade of political strategy from that applied in the established international community to the radicalism of policies used in Algeria during the struggle for independence (1954–1962) (Sulayman 1993:147). Such a framework, which he claims can be used to explain everything, ultimately explains little. Basically any policy pursued by any Muslim (not necessarily Islamic) country is justifiable in its own right rather than in light of Islamic principled beliefs. His exhortations that regimes should respect the moral dimensions of Islam simply fall in the realm of preaching rather than of policy action or inference. Values, ideas and beliefs matter not only as moral guidelines, but also as road maps particularly institutionalized as a decision–making determinant, even in the absence of a unique equilibrium. In an anarchic and in many ways hostile external environment Islamic theory and action is not solely guided by objective constraints and opportunities but also where selection from a range of viable outcomes is based on beliefs and expectations (Goldstein & Keohane 1993:17). Otherwise *unwillingness* to pursue a particular Islamic course of action or policy could be easily con-fused with '*inability*,' an example of which could be unity among two or more Muslim states entailing surrender of political incumbency. Thus, in addition to failing the explanatory test, Sulayman fails the parsimony test. In contrast to Prophet Muhammad, who is reported to have stated "I have been given the *parsimony* of words (*ouwtitu jawami' ul– kalim*)," or to Ibn Khaldun and his concept of *assabiyya*, or more recently to Grand Ayatollah Khomeini and his principle of *Wilayat al–Faqih*, Sulayman's framework provides no equivalents. Whereas the classical theory explains parsimoniously, that of Sulayman basically dis–integrates the whole subject matter.

Thirdly, the structure of the Islamic theory of nations reflected an "intersubjective conception" in which normative identities and cognitive interests were determined by processes *endogenous* to interaction, rather than exogenous to them as modern realism and institutionalism assume (Wendt 1992:391–392). At the same time, it incorporated a good measure of concern with issues of actor power and capabilities. However, it sought primarily to 'maximize' the 'spread' of the message of Islam as a religious 'given' rather than, the 'self–interested utility' of power or material welfare as a modern rationalist argument would suggest. The latter were considered contingent to the necessary former. Unlike functional approaches, beliefs are crucial guidelines even though actions based on their provisions may lead to no perceived gain in efficiency or material benefits for society at large (Goldstein & Keohane 1993:17). This is particularly true in cases where material losses constitute the price of spiritual and/or long run, sometimes, unobservable gain. The Islamic Republic of Iran for instance, would have perhaps been better off, from a rational self–interested point of view, if it were to support the Middle East 'peace' process and recognize Israel, instead of bringing upon itself the enmity of the United States with all that this entails. In reordering the elements of contingency and necessity, classical Islamic conceptions of world order cut across much of modern Western theoretical assumptions. In their *autonomous* capacity, they incorporated constants and continuities, though much less so change, which respectively and by extension combined the self–referential mechanisms of *retention* and *selection*, but also much less so *variation* (Teubner 1993:49 & 56). Despite the relative lack of dynamism due to the absence of change and variation — both hindered by the regression in the talents of *ijtihad* — it was *autonomy* and *self–referentiality* which embedded the theory in the *Shari'ah,* as well as the intrinsic structure of the theory itself. In other words, while the theory may not be identical with the *Shari'ah* as revelation, it cannot be separated from it as root and source.

Fourthly, the classical theory's binary opposition between the two abodes is methodologically consistent with corresponding and replete Islamic/Qur'anic binary categories.[9] Dispensing with it chips away at, and bears a negative impact on the *Shari'ah,* unless an alternative theoretical binary relationship can be constructed. One that is capable of isolating the normative boundaries within which ethical, religious, and political discourses are reasoned (Graham 1984:103). Furthermore, the principle of *reciprocity* makes up an integral component of the Islamic law of nations. It remains relevant particularly when in a globalization, perceived by many to be overtaking the

---

9   For example believers vs. unbelievers (4: 142); the deaf and the hearing (11: 25); those who see vs. those who are blind (40: 59); party of God vs. party of Satan (58 19 & 22), among many other binary opposites.

world, the Muslim *umma* is not a constitutive but rather constituted part of it, and perhaps much more so, its victim. This renders the external environment one of (neo) realism and anarchy, and not of interdependence, while necessitating a new kind of organic relationship among Muslim states. Given current global conditions, a conflictive state of affairs does in fact exist between two binary *abodes*. In contemporary parlance they are termed the North and the South, "Clash of Civilizations" (Huntington 1993), or "zones of peace" versus "zones of turmoil" (Singer & Wildavsky 1993:3). The dual categories exhibit an asymmetrical power relationship of durable inequality, between two worlds, that govern their interaction. A conflictive state in other words, is not necessarily one of hostility or antagonism *per se*, but the actual condition of structuration and asymmetry. Altering these conditions require a transformation in self–conception, which is no longer restricted by state boundaries, but transcended by universal Islamic values. The structure of the classical theory provides a relevant explanatory and potentially inferential framework, and a correspondence to an increasingly non–territorial world. In many ways in fact, it reflects reality and reciprocity.

Change in 'state' and concomitant self–conception, while not sufficient, remains a necessary condition for addressing the systemic durable inequality the modern state has·come to entrench. This is a problematic that Sulayman's adaptive approach does not seem to be able to tackle. It fails to deal with the fact that any system, which situates Muslims in a framework of durable inequality, directly opposes Islamic injunctions.[10] Values and beliefs must therefore focus the research agenda on how to reduce or eliminate this condition not how to adapt to it. Only subsequently are opportunities and constraints evaluated. Put differently,

---

10 "They say, "If we return to Medina, surely the more honourable (element) will expel therefrom the meaner." But *honour belongs to Allah and His Messenger, and to the Believers*; but the Hypocrites know not." (Qur'an 63:8; Translation by Yusuf Ali).

in an Islamic approach, ontology precedes and guides epistemology not the other way round, or alternatively as the classical Islamic theory has superbly done, sustains an enduring dialectical relationship between the two. When Sulayman attempted to separate the political aspects of the Islamic revelatory period (7th century AD) from the legal aspects (1993:97ff), he basically unraveled this connection. This was evident when he attempted to formulate the issue of legitimacy of the existence of diverse Muslim states under the rule of different rulers rather than just one '*Imam*,' seeking justification in references to some Muslim jurists (Sulayman 1993:37). Interpretive questions as to whether the 'oneness' of the Muslim *umma*, as referred to in the Qur'an, is spiritual or also political, is one example of how the manipulative formulation of a question could be such so as to invite polemical divergences and a break down in consensus. The Qur'anic verses making a reference to such unity (21:92; 23:52)[11] bear metaphorical/contingent meanings (*mutashabeh*), which require explanation by a higher categorical/necessary principle (*muhkam*). Yet, Sulayman misses the point. The question is not whether it is permissible to have only one or more Caliphs, rulers, or states, but whether or not the Muslim pseudo–states as they stand are sources of durable inequality. The former is a contingent question the latter requires a necessary resolution. Any doubts about the allegorical verse regarding the oneness of the Muslim *umma* may be resolved by the categorical Qur'anic principle "*honor belongs to Allah and His Messenger, and to the Believers*" (63:8). Many Muslims may seek to engage in opposing arguments regarding the spiritual or political unity of the *umma*. Few though would dissent as to whether a structure or system of "durable inequality" (Tilly 1999) is compatible with the situation of

---

11 "Verily, this community of yours is one community and I am your Lord, so worship ME" (Qur'an 21: 92; Translation by Yusuf Ali); "And know that this community of yours is one community, and I am your Lord. So take ME as your Protector" (Qur'an 23:52; Translation by Yusuf Ali).

honor to which the Qur'an entitles Muslims. The polemics that the allegorical verse could give rise to are, hence, resolved by a categorical principle. Such a 'hermeneutic' understanding would help in creating a good measure of consensus and in reformulating policy and structural issues in different and perhaps more productive, less polemical directions. The question is no longer the number of rulers but the *optimal* change in state structure, nature and content, which would allow for at least one Islamic *essential* actor capable of reciprocally influencing, participating and if need be, vetoing in the international and global system. Optimality and essentiality imply that while the bordered state and its colonial formative legacy must be transcended, it is not necessary nor required that there be only one Islamic State. This should not be perceived in any way as contradicting the basic Islamic principles of singularity, as too large a state could otherwise and depending on contingencies, prove more of a security burden contributing to more rather than to less inequality. This is so since variation in form, content and durability will depend on the nature of the resources involved, the previous political locations of the categories (formal status of state), the nature of the organizational problems, and the relative power and capability configurations of the actors involved (Tilly 1999:8). No longer, then, is it merely a question of having a democratically elected representative government with (neo)liberal commitments, but one of reformulating the meaning and horizons of the 'state.' Substantive issues of the kind pose both theoretical and practical revisionist challenges to the status quo particularly so as issues of identity come to the forefront.

Abstract proclamations for Islamic 'unity' and cooperation nevertheless, continue to be made essentially to cover up the need for actual policy guidelines, or to obscure the logical conclusions one must arrive at. Sulayman's de–politicizing approach contributes no inferential or predictive power in this respect. His call for Muslim "unity" (1993:161) does not go much beyond everyday rhetoric. Yet in examining the empirical cases of some policies such as the abandonment of war as the basis of foreign relations, adoption of diplomatic reciprocity and alliances with non– Muslim countries, and policies of neutrality, all are considered as legitimate even when contradictory (Sulayman 1993:147ff). How can the war option, for instance, be dropped by an *umma* living in an anarchic–realist world and invaded right in its heartland (for example Palestine, occupation of Iraq, Afghanistan and Somalia, deployment of forces in the Arabian Peninsula)? How could a policy, which effectively leads to the occupation of the Arabian Peninsula by American forces under the guise of 'alliance,' be equated with that of positive nonalignment? What are the standards, what are the constraints? As things stand in the Muslim world, *outside* systemic goals and objectives are being matched by the *inside* in an unbroken and undivided continuum of *interests*, *ideas*, and *structures*. Breaking this continuum in any one or all three is the challenge that the Muslim states will have to confront.

The crucial and central issue hence is to recognize and acknowledge *where*, in Khaldunian parlance, lies the *assabiyya* of Islam, who is most capable of reflecting it, and to coalesce around its representative, transcending territorial and vested or so called 'modern' state interests. It is the rational and the reasoned tackling of primarily political and strategic questions of the kind that will determine answers in light of which categorical provisions of the *Shari'ah* and determination of Islamic interests could be made. This requires an autonomous and self–referential re–conception of the highest intellectual and political magnitude and order. Policy decisions could then be set accordingly, and human and resource mobilization undertaken in a focused direction. Of all the states, Iran appears to be the sole credible *nucleus* state that holds out for such a prospect, and where a theory and structure of authority does exist.[12]It is more than a coincidence, that the only time and place where Israel has been forced to withdraw unconditionally from the Arab territory of South Lebanon in May 2000, and again bloodied militarily in July 2006 in its attempt to destroy the Lebanese Hezbollah, has been where the Iranian Islamic revolution had been relatively successfully exported. In light of the above, the Islamic theory or law of nations continues to play a positive religious and scholarly role in shaping and focusing Islamic consciousness. It further offers a new challenge to the intellectual capacities of Muslims and non–Muslims alike striving in a sincere effort not only to reconcile differences, but perhaps as importantly to explain them. The theory's contemporary relevance must therefore not be underestimated.

Reflections on the Sunni–Shi'i Controversy

The above begs the question of intra –Islamic relations, particularly those between the Sunnis and Shi'is. What follows does not attempt to dwell on Sunni–Shi'i polemics, political or *madhabi*, or try to resolve and reconcile their differences. Rather it endeavors to raise some points for brainstorming and heuristic purposes. Some may invoke the issue that Iran is mainly a Shi'i country and that it would be difficult therefore to garner needed support for its leadership of a majority Sunni Islamic world. To start with, it is worthwhile to refer to the famous fatwa made by the former head of al–Azhar University, Shaikh Mahmoud Shaltout, in 1959 that Shi'ism is a *madhab* as legitimate as its Sunni counterpart.[13] While

---

12   The Islamic theory of nations and Ibn Khaldun's theory together with the empirical experience of the Iranian Islamic revolution provide ample opportunity for broadening Muslims' intellectual horizons of research (*ijtihad*).

13   Al-Azhar Theological school in Egypt, one of the main centers of Sunni scholarship in the world announced the following on July 6, 1959: *"The Shi'a is a school of thought that is religiously correct to follow in worship as are other Sunni schools of thought."* On 6 July 1959, Shaikh

not all Sunnis have embraced this fatwa wholeheartedly, the barriers between both madhabs seem to be slowly yet steadily breaking down despite attempts by some parties (Salafi groups, the US, some Arab regimes) to continue to instigate sensitivities and rivalries for purposes of their own. In addition to the fact that more information about Shi'ism has been made available, particularly after the Iranian revolution's triumph and the sometimes grudging admiration if not envy, with which both Iran and Hezbollah are held.

Secondly, there tends to be a deep–seated disposition toward pointing fingers at the other side at the expense of self–reflection. A point which Sunnis strongly fault the Shi'a for, and to a good measure rightly so, is their sometimes offensive and critical language about some of the companions of the Prophet. However, it is also important to acknowledge that it was the Sunni Umayyad dynasty that had 'innovated' (ibtada'at) the habit of cursing Imam Ali and other members of the Prophet's household, as well as killing them. Yet they are rarely condemned as vociferously by the Sunnis, as the Shi'a have been. Granted this may be part of the past; however, an awareness of such historical facts may help dispose Muslims to put contemporary matters into *perspective*. Change and betterment remains always possible and preferable to futile mutual accusations. Mazaheb, after all, are derivatives (*branch*) from revelation or Shari'ah, and cannot therefore make claims to being

---

Mahmood Shaltoot the head of the al-Azhar Theological school-announced the al-Azhar Shia Fatwa: "1) Islam does not require a Muslim to follow a particular Madh'hab (school of thought). Rather, we say: every Muslim has the right to follow one of the schools of thought which has been correctly narrated and its verdicts have been compiled in its books. And, everyone who is following such Madhahib [schools of thought] can transfer to another school, and there shall be no crime on him for doing so.2) The Ja'fari school of thought, which is also known as "al-Shia al-Imamiyyah al-IthnaAshariyyah" (i.e. The Twelver Imami Shi'ites) is a school of thought that is religiously correct to follow in worship as are other Sunni schools of thought. Muslims must know this, and ought to refrain from unjust prejudice to any particular school of thought, since the religion of Allah and His Divine Law (*Shariah*) was never restricted to a particular school of thought. Their jurists (*Mujtahidoon*) are accepted by Almighty Allah, and it is permissible to the "non-Mujtahid" to follow them and to accord with their teaching whether in worship (*Ibadaat*) or transactions (*Mu'amilaat*)"(http://shiite-muslim.anime.co.za/anime/Shiite_Muslim).

intrinsic sources of ultimate truth. Otherwise, they would be making the same claim as the origin and source revelation (*stem*), which would put them in a contradictory rather than consistent relationship. While most Muslims may be willing to concede this point, much of their actions belie their claims. Moreover, where a madhab might err in one point, it may show rectitude and insight in another, and vice versa. This is the case, for example, when Sunnis have largely invested authority and legitimacy in *political* power, even though they like to deny it, while the Shi'a invested both in *moral* power. By justifying the corrupt state and its tyranny, or at best making peace with it, the Sunni madhab undermined the principle of *Justice* and, over time, its *ulama*, deservedly so, lost much of their credibility, unlike their Shi'i counterparts.[14] This set the latter to be more qualified to lead than the former, as Sunni clerics tend to lack the knowledge, aptitude, aura or respectability which rendered their Shi'i opposite numbers more dynamic, authoritative, and capable of transcending emulative tradition. In other words, the Sunni madhabi field appears to be only capable of producing *pseudo-ulama or* clerics not only due to their shortcomings, but as significantly, due to their lack of independence, both as emulators, and as state as well as foreign instruments.[15]

---

14 "When We decide to destroy a population, We (first) send a definite order to those among them who are given the good things of this life and yet transgress; so that the word is proved true against them: then (it is) We destroy them utterly" (Qur'an 17:16). (www.IslamicCity.com). Whether possibly being offensive about some companions of the Prophet, for reasons which go back to historical conflicts in early Islamic history, is worse or less so than undermining the principle of Justice, is moot. However, the following Qur'anic verse may provide a hint: "Allah loveth not that evil should be noised abroad in public speech, except where injustice hath been done; for Allah is He who heareth and knoweth all things" (Qur'an 4:148; www.IslamiCity.com). If the Shi'a feel they had been subjected to historical injustices they have a right to voice their grievances as well as to identify who they believe to have inflicted such injustices on them. It may serve presenting their case better however, if they avoid any impropriety in this respect. By the same token, Sunnis in turn, should quit pretensions that no historical errors have been committed and that it was all a matter of *ijtihad*, especially that much of the Muslim World today is still living the consequences of this erroneous 'ijtihad.' As Imam Ali has said, "know men by righteousness not righteousness by men." In any case, given the challenges that the Muslim world is facing, it may be best to manifest an ability to transcend such problems, in word as well as in deed, particularly when they are being rehashed and manipulated by both domestic and external enemies.

15 Joseph Braude, who worked for the CIA, observed that "politically ambivalent" and "liberal" Sunni ulama in the Gulf states of Bahrain, the UAE and Kuwait, not to mention Egypt, "tend

Independence is a *necessary* condition of knowledge (*ilm*). Where there is no independence or freedom, there is no *ilm*, in the same vein of the principle: there is 'no authority for a prisoner' (*la wilayat li 'aseer*). One may also add and, *no ijtihad for a hired hand* (*la ijtihad li 'ajeer*), at least in general and broad terms, not precluding exceptions.

The point here is not to deny that there have been worthy Sunni scholars. Rather, it is to focus attention on the outcome of the general interaction between the State and the ulama, over time and space, which came to be embedded in Sunni Muslim consciousness. How this impacted on the Muslim and Islamic condition, notwithstanding some figure or *'alim* here or there making a firm stand against State injustices. And what implications did this have on the Sunni madhab and its *fiqh sultani* — the Islamic jurisprudence or discourse justifying state power. Was *fiqh sultani* the indirect means by which *al–Mulk al–Adud*, failing to present itself in positive light, yet seriously concerned about Shi'i opposition, manipulated both faith and ulama to divide the umma so as to safeguard itself against unified opposition? Aware that mere *political* accusations and repression of the Shi'a might not garner necessary resonance among the masses at large, was a madhabi twist using religious sentiments — which finds its contemporary most radical manifestation among *salafi* and Wahhabi groups — perhaps the State's answer? Was it a matter of formulating the problematic in a particular conceptual framework rather than another? These points are not to be taken lightly nor are they simply rhetorical questions. For when the principle of *Justice*, in all its aspects and dimensions had been forsaken, Muslims sought refuge elsewhere in secular codes, which undermined Islamic values. In the barrenness and desolation of their condition, Muslims became vulnerable to the combined assault of democracy, (neo)liberalism and human rights, the three pronged components of secularism. The net effect has

---

to be hard pressed for cash" (Braude 2003:71). The intimation is there for all to read.

been something similar to what an Arab poet had once said about wine: "...Heal me with what has been the malady;" wine being the source of both his depressing hang–over, as well as his exuberant high. One recurring state invites the other, entrapping him in the vicious circle of mental and psychological dependency, the same dependency which secularism imposed on Muslim societies, added to it the cultural component.[16] In both cases, the alcoholic does not transform his reality, though his high may make him feel so for a time until reality sets in again. On a broader scale, neither does the Muslim umma change much. As a matter of fact, the more it seems to change the more things turn out to be the same. In Algerian thinker Malek bin Nabi's words, they became subject to a condition of 'susceptibility' to colonialism.

It is of concern therefore, despite strong resurgence in Islamic religious sentiments that Sunni *pseudo-ulama* and movements, instead of having learned their lessons, end up making a comeback with the same loaded baggage of historical fiascoes. This time additionally vindicated by what they perceive to be the failure of the modern secular project in the Arab world. Hopefully this does not turn out to be a situation where nothing has been learned and nothing has been forgotten, to recall Tallyrand's words about the Bourbons. Alternatively, *knowledgeable* Muslims on both sides of the Sunni–Shi'i divide may consider some form of madhabi *synthesis* in order to attain a higher level of Islamic consciousness capable of saving the 'baby' so to speak, while

---

16   Such a condition borders on a form of pathological *xenophilia* where any and everything coming from the 'other,' in this case mostly the West, is better, even if this may not be the case. Muslims have been strictly forewarned about such a state in the *hadith* where Prophet Muhammad says to the effect: "you shall follow the ways [*sunan*] of those before you [Jews and Christians] foot step by foot step, were they to enter a lizard's pit you shall follow in" (author's translation). This does not in any way indicate that there is nothing of value to learn from other nations or people. After all, the Prophet is also reported to have said "seek knowledge even in China (read end of the world)." Rather, the former hadith refers to the collapse in the faculty of discernment, and the failure of distinguishing and differentiating capacities, that many Muslims will come to suffer from. Essentially it refers to lack of good judgment. One may add that such failures of judgment could be a product of xenophilia, as well as its opposite extreme, xenophobia.

doing away with the dirty water. This ought to constitute a different and future looking *strategic* project that avoids the burdens of historical grievances, actual or perceived, biases and prejudices. These reflections, which I pose heuristically and as potential road maps for further examination, call as well for collective archeological excavation of the real nature and dynamics of the historical relationship between Islamic *mazaheb*, *politics* and the *state*. This could be done by constructing a common Sunni–Shi'i framework within which such a relationship may be examined and the process of excavation undertaken.

A second set of heuristic reflections relates to the religio–philosophical meaning of change *within* 'family' branches. This is particularly significant as symbolized by the historical shift in the prophethood line from that of the Israelites to that of the Ismaelites (the Arabs). The Israelites were the chosen people of God (Qur'an 2:47; 2:122) yet, when their work proved them unworthy (Qur'an 2:83), the kingdom of God was taken from them and given to another people or nation, to use biblical language (Mathew 21:43).[17]

When Prophet Muhammad declared the message of Islam (610 AD), and called also upon the Jews of Medina to believe in the new faith, he essentially was calling upon them — using social theory's non–religious language — to 'reconceptualize' (read both *renounce* and *confirm*) their long held beliefs in favor of an Islam that would bring them back to their own pristine message. The moral of this *analogical* historical experience may be relevant today, although on a reduced dimension.[18] Whereas Jews of the time were presented

---

17 Islam upholds this position, and the following discussion is based on such an Islamic belief and understanding of events. It is important to note that no nation is given a 'blank check' so to speak. In this respect the Prophet is reported to have said to the effect: Let people not come [on the Day of Judgment] with their works and you [the Arabs] come with kinship and status (author's translation).

18 Qur'anic narrations (*qasas*) are not merely a recounting of religiously significant events which had transpired, but are at the same time 'prophecies' and 'news' as to what is to occur in the future, in analogical equivalences. This perhaps is why Prophet Muhammad, describing the Qur'an, is reported to have said "... in it are recounts about those before you, and the 'news/prophecies' of that which is after you ... (*fihi khabar man qablakumwa naba'a ma ba'dakum*

with the stark choice of having to change their religion, Muslims, and Sunnis in particular, mercifully, need only 'reconceptualize' interpretations, opinions, methodologies, nuances, as well as prejudices — the constructing elements of mazaheb as they have come to stand. Sunni Muslims need to develop a reflexive mind–set regarding some of their long cherished opinions and their attitudes vis–à–vis the Madhabi branch of their Shi'i brethren. For resting content in their 'orthodoxy' is a luxury they could ill afford. The point here is not to be construed as some call for a collective madhabi change. Rather it is an appeal for self–reflection among the Sunni majority, as to what their madhab, apart of mere ritualism, could still offer. Whether it has reached some kind of an impasse or dead end and whether it has become a burden on Islam instead of the facilitator it was supposed to be. What does it have to offer socially, politically, institutionally and from thereon morally i.e. in terms of Islamic politics rather than merely politics of Islam?

It is also a call for pondering Iranian leadership of the umma, notwithstanding *madhabi* considerations. Especially so, when the Arab state itself has reached a parallel impasse and dead end, not only as a corrupt and tyrannical regime structure, but taking matters a step further, as a *corruptor* and destroyer of values, deprived essentially of its *raison d'etre*.

Al–Mulk al–Adud and *fiqh sultani,* the two components of the historical ideology of *sunn–ism* incorporating politics of Islam — the ideological aspect of the broader Sunni madhab — or any of their variations (for example *hukm jabri* or rule by force) are unlikely to have the means, methods,

---

...). Thus for instance, where Jews are condemned by the Qur'an for killing the Prophets of God, The Qur'an in effect was also stating that Muslims,though on a reduced 'analogical' dimension, being a *blessed* nation (*umma marhouma*)and therefore immune from committing a 'capital' sin, will perpetrate a *parallel* crime and kill the Prophet's-grandson (for example Imam Hussain) and other members of the Prophet's household. Or, when the *people of the book* are accused of corrupting their *revealed* scriptures, Muslims again, on a reduced scale, commit parallel corruption *interpreting* their Qur'anic and/or *hadith* scriptures (as manifested for example in *fiqh sultani*) — the Qur'an itself, being immune from corruption, and many ulama, though by no means all, being not much different from the condemned rabbis of the children of

will or capacity to remedy or address these problems. In addition, by continuously reproducing a class of religious sycophants, charlatans and emulators (*muqallidin*) lacking in *praxis* knowledge on one hand, a dogmatic *salafi* mentality on the other, and a forlorn majority in between infused with a spirit of submissiveness to ruling power whatever its nature, as a matter of 'religious' obligation, *sunnism* has effected an Islamic pathological condition which permeated all levels of Muslim society. To the extent that some Sunnis sought to challenge this state of affairs they largely had to resort to the marginal and anarchist thought of the Kharijites. Perhaps this 'empirical' observation is consistent with and a sound hint towards understanding the Qur'anic, and Prophetic tradition concerning 'Divine substitution' (*istibdal*) (Qur'an 47:39; See also note 5). In fact, it might very well be the case that if Sunnis were to try to ensure the effective survival of their madhab, that they capitalize on the burst of energy and dynamism of its *Ja'fari* Shi'i counterpart, as well as on that of the Iranian revolutionary experience instead of conspiring against it. When Abdullah II of Jordan made his alarmist statement in 2005 about a 'Shi'ite Crescent' threat to the region, and with king Abdullah of Saudi Arabia being groomed for an 'ambiguous' role as leader of the American sponsored *unholy* alliance of 'Sunni moderates,' comprising the former two countries plus Egypt, the foreboding signs are there to see. It is perhaps this reality which prompted the leading Egyptian journalist and political analyst Muhammad Hassanein Heikal, commenting on the historical pattern of American–Arab relations to indicate that this 'game' between the "swindler and the buffoons" has gone way too long (Heikal 26 April 2007). It further raised the fundamental and existential question about who and "what saved the [umma] when the ruler[s] offered catastrophic leadership or none at all" (Knox 1996:616)?

Israel. Such proposed 'prophetic' dimensions of *qasas* call perhaps for further investigation. See also the hadith of the *sunan* above (footnote 15).

Even when Arab regimes claim that they are concerned about the 'political,' not the madhabi project of Iran, and that Iran has a nationalist agenda involved, it is important to note that Islam does not mean the absence of strategy, politics or interests. One does not negate the others. As a matter of fact, it is reflection of the genius of a people or a civilization when either is capable of reconciling or *appropriating* otherwise potentially conflicting values (i.e. Islamic politics and politics of Islam). For instance, early Muslim armies' zeal to spread the faith did not prohibit spoils taking, nor did the religious duty of pilgrimage proscribe engagement at the same time in legitimate worldly concerns or benefits (Qur'an 22:27–28). Compare this with the unfortunate and largely unnecessary conflicts that occurred, in the contemporary Arab world, between nationalist and religious currents, and then each current within itself. Arabs may also recall that they had been once 'substituted' by the Sunni Ottoman Turks, in terms of loss of political power. If they ally themselves with the US or Israel in order to *allegedly* protect both their *interests* and *madhab* (politics of Islam) they may effectively lose their soul as well as end up wasting both of the former objectives, [19] and deserving of '*substitution*' (Islamic politics). For in the end it is not madhabi *constructions*, which matter most, when the ultimate Islamic criterion of judgment is clear: "Verily the most honoured of you in the sight of Allah is (he who is) righteous of you. And Allah has full knowledge and is well acquainted (with all things)" (Qur'an 49:13; www.IslamiCity.com).

---

19 As far back as 2007, Issam No'man indicated in *Al–Quds Al–Arabi* Newspaper, published in the UK, that based on information from high level American officials, the US has been arming Sunni radical groups in Lebanon, in order to instigate a Sunn–Shi'i conflict and to attack Hezbollah, while blaming al-Qaida for the violence (18 April 2007). It seems that the US together with some Arab states and parties are following the same manipulative tactics with these groups as they did earlier during the Afghan War (1979-1989). The final targets, no doubt, are Iran and Syria (as events show), against which the US has been working hard to build an Arab/Sunni–Israeli alliance.

Comment

Prof. Dr. Ahmet Çiğdem (Türkei)

Under the title "Islamic Politics or Politics of Islam" Amr Sabet presents us, albeit in an unrefined ground, a body of ideas scattered out through his text, with the aim in responding to the question of how an understanding of the *political* in Islam could be possible, and how such an understanding can be conceptually developed as it is inscribed in the very structure of the religion. He prefers obviously *a* politics of Islam to maintain the normative foundations of the Islamic political: a politics based upon the notions *assabiyya* and *wilayat al-faqih* to save religion as, and in itself against politicization of Islam, which could be possible as an instrumentalization of religion, a divergence either in terms of developing an exclusively political understanding of Islam in which the religion can only be a secondary factor, affirming an existing and pre-defined hegemonic frame, or religion has been emptied of its political content by -again- an exclusive religious interpretation, totally focusing upon the construction of religion only as *belief*. He clearly states that conceptual and theoretical aporias exist in such an undertaking. The problematization of issues and the search for alternatives are Amr Sabet's intentions, rather than presenting a rigid yet fragile political mapping, as I understand. The background to that discussion involves a set of problems, and each of them should be analysed in detail, he argues. The broad picture surrounding the problematique of politics and Islam is, first of all, related to the internal condition of the Muslim World. Saudi Arabia and

Iran are his two starting points to discuss the internal context as a state of disarray. Then, on the external condition
of the Muslim world, underlying the need for "a theory of
governance, as a prerequisite of a broader Islamic theory
of international relations", he mainly discusses Abu-Sulay-
man's views (1993),[1] who serves for him, as an integralist
figure, degrading Islam of its value, unloading the history
of Islam and thus, surrendering it to the logic of *realpoli-
tik*, the logic that annihilates Islamic spirit. The last part
of the presentation is about the sunni-shiite controversy.
The semi-religious differences and actual conflicts are to be
resolved rather than stigmatized and absolutized, in accor-
dance with the common religious sentiment, he concludes.

I wish I were able to understand Sabet's priorities, but,
unfortunately, I must confess that I have many problems
with his presentation and, to tell the truth, the question
he problematizes is not a convincing one, it appears, for a
number of reasons, lacking an essential dimension to which
one should refer to discuss the *problematique politique* in Islam. The text, this is only my subjective view I must stress,
cannot easily be thematized, it has so many things to say
but they remain unsaid in the very end, I claim, and therefore I will limit myself to an overall evaluation.

＾ 1. To begin with: Schmitt's concept of politics is a
multi-layered one, and cannot be used merely to indicate
that politics only involves, nor should involve, in taking decisions to make clear-cut distinctions between friend and
enemy in order to raise the authenticity and particularity
claims of a collective subject in action. Schmitt later re-ex-
amined his understanding of the political to the extent that
the original formulation was almost abandoned. The book,

---

1 *Towards an Islamic Theory of International Relations*, Herndon: The International Institute
of Islamic Thought. There is not much to say about choosing such a weak text to discuss, after
all, for instance, didn't Althusser pick John Lewis his interlocutor among so many strong and
well-established critics? But, I personally claim, this is almost a categorical imperative, that
the question of Islam cannot be discussed through and with, and in a context emphasizes semi-
managerial language of governance or international religions.

Der Begriff der Politischen, to my knowledge, has four different editions (1927, 1932, 1933, and 1963). The last edition, which is identical with the second edition, remains untouched, and was so compiled by Schmitt with the addition of extra materials that the book gained a different momentum: politics and state are no longer reducible to each other; they are historical and, thus objectively separated. Before 1963, there was an entwinement of state and politics, but the critical instance for the political was the distinction between friend and foe in which the foe was constructed almost ontologically. In 1963 edition, Schmitt still believes the state's omnipotence in defining the political, thus the foe, but the foe is no longer something ontological, it is legalized, it has now almost materialized as a unit. Finally, Schmitt declares at the end of *Jus Publicum Europeum* that a new nomos of the earth would inevitably take place (*Nomos der Erde*). The political, state, friend and foe cannot be understood in their modern appearances. Because the *nomos* they have to obey has just changed with the disempowering of *Jus Publicum Europeum* by *Pax Americana*.

The supremacy of state, as he exemplified in his *Verfassunglehre* at the same period that the concept (*Der Begriffe des Politischen*) was formulated, is the basic tenet of Schmitt's political position. The polemos between friend and foe presupposes two different homogenous bodies in the form of friend and enemy which are meaningful not in themselves but only in relation to the state. Having understood that confining politics to society and individuals is a liberal illusion, why do we have to stay with the idealistic fallacy that covers politics by the state? And the point is that any politics in search of such homogeneous units as such, in my view, clearly conflicts with a project of open and emancipatory social imagination. I don't think even the Islamic one, if we consider the social and its spheres, in the advanced global capitalist machine, can attempt at having such a homogeneous body. That is clearly totalitarianism in the very sense of the word. Pluralism is not an impudent child for the so-called post-modern, post-state, post-nation societies; it is a *factum socius* of modern societal existence. Last but not least, Schmitt's political is content-less. From the most radical to the integrationist, any kind of Islamic politics would be value-laden. In other words, a politico-theological notion of politics would always include ultimate ends, it cannot be established alongside opportunistic and utilitarian principles.

2. From here, I dare to argue that this use of Ibn Khaldun's concept of *assabiyya* would also be misleading. This is not denying the sociological function and meaning of the concept. The hiatus between phenomena and noumena can still be explained by *assabiyya* in every sociological and historical level that it can almost perfectly perform a kind of Khaldunian a priori in the construction of the social. But the use of *assabiyya* as an other-directed ideological device in the formation of Muslim identities, as a prerequisite of Islamic politics could only result for a search of authenticity and perfection, which no politics can afford to bring in. The usage of the concept in an exclusionary manner that it is being invested in particular people, or in a specific religious understanding and practice, cannot be justified in any circumstances. This requires a particularization of religion, an act of destructing its universality. The author's own preference for Iran is understandable that Iran implies something political which other Muslim states do not. But the equation of state and society with the name "Iran" or "Saudi Arabia" is simply wrong. The total control of society by the state does not legitimize to blend state and society within the same melting pot, and, in this respect, Iran and Saudi Arabia are very similar to each other and, yes, it is an external critique in the form of fundamentalism, but this similarity has become possible through the medium of authoritarianism. *Assabiyya*, be it invested or not, does not change the nature of political regime. The hereditary totalitarianism in Saudi

Arabia is replaced by a dictatorship of Islamic nomencla-
ture in Iran. Peoples of respective societies are not eligible
to come into the scene as totalitarian, and apart from their
self-constituting claims, it would be injustice to label them
as such. Let me indicate the point that there is a huge difference between reconstructing the concept of *assabiyya* at
theoretical level and having assabiyya in the socio-political
sphere.

Unfortunately, the same approach is also valid for the
concept *Wilayat al-Fakih*; for it legitimizes the political tu-
telage, first; then, it monopolizes society by law whether it
is divine or human. In both cases, society is submitted to
either a supreme reason or a supreme principle. The truth is
that the submissiveness of the social to law, the reduction
of societal to juridicial reason can only be carried out under
the force of omnipotent will which lies outside the historical. From there to fascism there is only one easy step.

3. In relation to Turkey: the AKP (Adalet ve Kalkın-
ma Partisi, Justice and Development Party) is not following open hidden religious politics, never did, as far as I can
see, nor does it have a hidden agenda of Islam, quite the
opposite: AKP is trying to build a conservative scheme of
democracy, and it is limited, it is lacking the very democratic element of struggle. For the moment, AKP seems to
be more conservative and liberal than being democrat if we
measure the performativity. This is the most democratic
phase of contemporary Turkish history at the very end of
day. The lesson I have learnt even from the AKP example:
Where and whenever democracy, even with its worst appearances, comes into play, there and then surprisingly,
an Islamic formation has been born and developed in the
Islamic part of the world. Instead of an endless and almost
useless discussion of the given and limited conditions of
democracy, (but please let us not miss the point: this is still
a huge problem) wouldn't it be more functional to empha-
size the democratic cause?

4. In relation to the dilemma between *Islamic Politics* and *Politics of Islam*: Sabet might be right to insist on the essential difference among those pair of concepts. I respect that. But we have to rethink the concept of political Islam in order to see why it is dangerous, sometimes, to be caught up in nominalism: There was, not so long ago, a conflict between cultural and political Islam. Those who are in a desperate mood to clean Islam from its "political" distortions, I mean moderate people like Bassam Tibi, convinced us that the survival of Islam could only be possible in the acceptance of religion as culture. But we all know (and better accept) the fact that religion without culture is spiritless (*Geistlos*), religion without the political would inevitably result in religion without community (*Gemeinschaftlos*). Though religion defended by political Islam resembled an infantile disorder, it contributed to the existence of Islamic community. I am ready to agree with Sabet that politics of Islam is instrumentalization of religion, in some cases, an open manipulation, maybe a total mobilization of Muslim masses in one-sided streets, I am even reluctant to give credit to the petit social movements in the struggle for a politics of Islam. But the failure implies another possibility of emancipation, there should be, the failure says, different ways to truth than the one we had already exhausted. The master who raises his hands to condemn the failed one is not exempt from the banality of error.

Why don't we use, for instance, instead of Schmitt, this is just an example, Benjamin's politico-theological *Bildung* of religion that wishes religion to be a religion of suffering, a religion for the suffered. Religion is not a source of eternal happiness and power. We are not the sovereign of the earth, just the opposite: we are just simple guests. Apart from justice and equality, and freedom (especially being free of external pressure of worldly authorities) we have no value to tell us what to do. We have no other criteria that will guide us in this struggle of survival in the postmodern world. This is the modest formulation of our contemporary reality, regardless of its being evaluated as "occidental." The measure is plain: the tears of a single individual that arise from grief and poverty cannot be redeemed by a successful social engineering through politics. Being a Muslim should mean being the conscience of the world, if we want to universalize our condition in the present situation, but unfortunately from conscience, no social or political order would emanate, but only and possibly a humble minima moralia. And this is not only a political issue, so there will be no exclusive political solution for the questions we have, just like a philosophical one would not be convincing either. So we have so many ways to go before we take the simple decision which asserts we are there.

Debates on Islam in the Public Sphere and their Impact on the Muslims' Perception of their Religion

Prof. Dr. Stefano Allievi (Italien)

Chaotic concepts – hidden order?

Even if it is undoubtedly true that a 'postmodern' and 'globalized' society is characterized by "complexity, contingency, confusion, chaos, and crisis", as it is written in the introduction to the present International Symposium, it is also true, nevertheless, that chaos often hides, on a different level, a hidden order. Complexity at the macro level conceals a certain number of simpler phenomena at the micro level. What is confusion for some is often the visible image of what is clarity for others (typically for those who know what it is happening, those who have relevant information, those who have originated a certain phenomenon). Contingency is not so unstable as it is often perceived. To conclude, crisis is often just another way to name life, with its difficulties, problems and their solutions.

This is very evident, for instance, when we try to analyze modern cities, which are a perfect metaphor for modern societies: the superficial images of chaos we perceive (traffic jams, apparent disorder of movements, etc.) hide in reality the superposition of different orders. The metaphor is clearer if we imagine to superpose, to the map of a city, different contact papers with: different populations (in terms of age, sex, job, religion, ethnic origin, etc.) of the city and their respective meeting points and itineraries, maps of public transport, of electricity cables, of telephone connections, of public institutions with their different publics, of schools, of commuters and other city users, etc. – all the different sub-systems and 'tribes' that live in or are related to a city. Every map has an internal order: but when we superpose all of them the image we have is that of confusion. We see a global chaos: but the subsystems in themselves are often a relatively ordered cosmos.

What I mean by using this metaphor is that, often, chaos and confusion is the superficial impression or description of an understandable 'different' order: it is enough, to understand the problem, to look 'behind', or a little more 'in depth'. What many of us perceive and understand as chaos, is a situation created by someone else, maybe at a different level and for different purposes: it is the case, often, of conflicts (including so called cultural conflicts). They are perceived, in the common opinion, as negative, a kind of disorder; but for some – typically the 'entrepreneurs of conflict', those who have something to gain from them – it is a positive and advantageous situation: a different level of order. And in many cases, as we will see, conflict is a physiological situation, a necessary phase of transition, a step towards a new and different order.

This is probably the case of the "Muslims' distorted perception of the self and of the world". For instance, of the debates in the public sphere about Islam and Muslims, and of the self- perception Muslims have of themselves and their religion.

In this sense, does chaos *really* exists or is it the effect – eventually, in Boudon's terms, a perverted effect – of a certain number of perfectly rational (in Weber's definition of rationality, which is not limited to the economic one) and not disordered actions?

I will divide my considerations in two parts that constitute more or less the two halves of the title that has been proposed to me: a) Debates on Islam in the public sphere; b) Muslims' perception of their religion (in Europe).

Debates on Islam in the public sphere

The immigrant and the Muslim: salience of religious categories

The other, the different, the foreigner, the immigrant. And today the Muslim. A path that has unravelled in the course of the decades and which in particular has transformed one category into the other, through a semantic shift and a selective perception of not little importance, which corresponds only in part to real changes.

If in fact right from the years of the post-War reconstruction and the economic boom it was the category of the immigrant that prevailed, from the 70s, and in a more decisive manner afterwards (with many differences according to the country, and the respective migratory situation) the Muslim became increasingly visible, for many reasons.

We can quite rightly say that the immigrants coming from Muslim countries brought Islam with them, in their suitcases. But for many years they left it there: not only were they not perceived as Muslims (the Turks in Germany were just Turks, the Indo-Pakistanis in Great Britain only immigrants from former colonies, as were Algerians in France – and everywhere in Europe classification, perception and also study were limited to ethnic and national variables), but they considered themselves essentially immigrants, transitory to boot (the weight of the "myth of the return" in all this, typical of the first generations of immigrants, should be considered). Their Islam, the weight of the religious variable, all the more so if lived collectively and in a community, was, all things considered, secondary: Islam, if it was there, often remained in the suitcases, or at most was relegated to the private sphere, with few exceptions.

In central-northern Europe the turning point came in the 70s when, following on from the oil crisis and the consequent economic crisis, immigrants began to realise that they would have to consider their presence in Europe as no longer transitory, but definitive. Or, more brutally put, they found themselves faced with the alternative of returning home, which would make it impossible for them to re-enter Europe (in the wake of almost universal progressive approval of more restrictive immigration laws, which would effectively put an end to their previous continuous comings and goings), and a definitive acceptance of their European horizon, with the consequent need to put down roots, including culturally – in addition to following the presence of those who are wrongly called second generations but which, not having ever moved, are actually the first generation of neo-autochthones.

In Southern European countries, the situation was different and the shift happened lately and differently. Italy, Spain and others became countries of immigration only in the 70s after having been for more than a century countries of emigration. For them, the change was even stronger and more rapid. They too passed through the stage of sole ethnicisation of immigration (perceived on the basis of the countries or areas of origin). But the stage of Islamisation of immigration, to use a deliberately strong expression, came more quickly, even instantaneously with the first generations, without waiting for a second generation towards which they would feel the need to transmit their cultural and religious capital. Mosques, in short, and everything that revolves around them, seemed to play in these countries an even more important role, if only because highlighted by the inadequacy or weakness of other interlocutors (included associative, ethnic, cultural, secular, etc.), than they do in other European countries.

So, even if it seems strange if seen with the eyes of the present cultural debate, there was a time, not so far off, when Muslims in Europe were *only* immigrants. Why has the situation changed? There are internal reasons connected with the world of migrations we have already seen. Then there are reasons connected with the emergence of Islam as a disruptive element, also on the symbolic plane: as a global geo-political actor (from the local crises connected with Islam – Afghanistan, Algeria, Bosnia, Palestine, Chechnya. Iraq and many others – up to trans-national Islamic terrorism and the impact of the terrorist attack upon the Twin Towers and, then, still in the West, the attacks upon Madrid and London); as an instrument and interpretative category (from Huntington onwards, in a very widespread literature, above all in its more popular versions); as a social and political actor of ever greater importance also in the countries of origin of the European immigrants; as a factor and an actor of growing importance in receiving countries, as an internal minority, occasionally visibilized through conflicts (Theo Van Gogh's murder, the Danish cartoons, recurrent debates on the veil and on mosques, etc.).

But there are also long-term reasons (the deep currents, to use an expression dear to Braudel, more important, even if less observed, than the *histoire événementielle*, which does not represent anything but the froth on the surface waves), internal to the European West, which do not have to do only with Islam, but more in general with tendencies of religions as a whole. The last thirty years, in particular, have led to a radical transformation in the religious field in various European countries: which have become (all, even those traditionally religiously monopolists like Catholic Italy and Spain), on the religious level, more and more plural. This process has taken place for two reasons: a process of pluralisation inside the dominant religious field (whether Catholic or Protestant), and a progressively greater presence of other religions, or of other ways of being religious, as well as non-religious options, or of abandonment of the religious field altogether.

This second element of pluralisation was in turn due to two tendencies: an internal pluralisation, autochthonous, produced in the resident population; and the arrival of allochthonous populations, with religions different from those already present in the country (and at times different *ways* of belonging to the same religions).

If the *fact* of progressive religious pluralisation can be considered both as a fact and a tendency in progress, it has not being *perceived* as such to the same degree: the public, media and political discourse on religion has remained still essentially very close to the dominant religious institutions of the majority religions (or too hastily identified as such). This change in the religious field took place in a period that, in contrast to other periods in the recent history of Europe, was seeing religion ever more present in the public discourse, for reasons connected as much with processes of globalisation and their cultural consequences, as the effect of media visibility that only had in part the same origins.

In speaking about Islam, why am I referring to a more general and undifferentiated pluralisation of the religious field? Because I have the very strong feeling that in public discussion Islam has taken on a crucial role among other religions, as, in a certain sense, it represents the *extreme case* (or to be precise, the case perceived, rightly or wrongly, as the more extreme) of pluralisation itself: discussion of and on Islam, with the historical and symbolic overload it carries with it, reassumes and in a certain sense replaces discussion about pluralisation, which has taken place and is on the increase, but is not at all understood and even less digested, metabolised, by the social body.

How and when the immigrant became a Muslim

In the last thirty years, as we have seen, a new element of reflection and a new analytical point of view has burst onto the scene: privileging reflection of a cultural nature, specifically religious. At the risk of producing a new reductionism, immigrants has been considered more as Muslims, and less as workers, students, parents, children, refugees, etc.: the starting point of reflection and public discussion has shifted from the roles they have to their (pre-supposed) identities. This has been a way to re-introduce the category not only of diversity, but also of otherness, if not of extraneousness, and even, as a consequence that is sometimes theorised, of incompatibility, in situations in which it was no longer verifiable and demonstrable from other points of view (it is enough to refer, as an example, to second generations: no longer immigrants, less and less 'other', always less different – but, when "Islamised", they re-become 'other' and different and even extraneous, according to the interpretations).

This kind of debate has started outside academia and social research: in debates that are invading the public space, in politics, in the media, in certain religious considerations, in many popular essays. But it also affects sociology strongly. As a response to a lack, an underestimation, that might be considered indecent and most unscientific, of the cultural and religious element, in many sociological approaches, such as labour analysis or the race relations approach. And as an element of a new, subtle and (more) powerful form of xenophobia. The literature that sees the Muslim as different, the 'other', at times the enemy (mostly extra- sociological, it must be said), is spreading. The best sold books on Islam often belong to a literature of this kind.

One of the paradoxes of this situation is that today, when we find ourselves in a not-simple moment of transition between an Islam *in* Europe and an Islam *of* Europe (with signs already of the construction of an *European* Islam), it seems that the situation of the Islamic presence could be synthesized with this slogan: substantial integration, conflictual perception. Substantial integration is what we see in the labour market, in school, in cities:

where Muslims succeed or fail at the same standard of other immigrants. Conflictual perception is what the cultural (or sub-cultural) debate reveals: in a significant part of the media, in the political milieu, but also in parts of the cultural and religious establishment.

On the one hand we have the normality of immigration with its problems, its failures and its successes, on the other hand the exceptional nature of how a *specific* immigration and presence is perceived (which is not found in similar forms and modes with other immigrations, even if they are not less 'different' that the Islamic one in respect to European history). It is obvious that the exceptionality of the interpretation has many good reasons on its side, which come to us mainly from the present geo-political situation and the growth of trans-national Islamic terrorism's capacity to strike (the West and its public imagination). But it is equally true that this does not explain everything. The conflictual interpretation of the Islamic presence in Europe, and the spread of a popular Huntingtonian interpretation of the "clash of civilizations", in fact *precedes* September 11, 2001, and we find it in the press, in conflicts over the *hijab* or in urban conflicts concerning mosques and cemeteries, as well as in political parties and religious movements and public discussions which had chosen Islam as a target well before the attack on the Twin Towers.

So the problem precedes geo-politics and terrorism, and has profound roots and a symbolic overload that must be held in consideration. Only this can explain the fierceness of certain attitudes to Islam circulating in the European public space, in which sometimes it would suffice to substitute the word "Jew" for the word "Muslim" to understand their gravity and negative potentiality. Naturally, in this process of demonising Islam, a more general process of *social construction of fear* plays a crucial role, which is part of the more general transformation of our society into a "risk society", in Beck's terms. A fear whose general meaning is now a "long-term tendency" of the contemporary West, from which many draw advantage, and whose specific anti-Islamic aspect is also creating advances in political and intellectual positions, and extremely concrete economic profits (conflict and demonization – included Islamophobia – sells much better than any dialogue of civilisations or religions).

Reactive Identities and Conflicts on Islamic symbols in the European public space

In this phase, in which the interpretative paradigms (also those of common discourses, not only the scientific ones) are still weak and little attested, identity conflicts and reactive identities are emerging. By reactive identities I mean identities that exist (particularly in public) only in opposition to someone else's identity, which is presupposed more than demonstrated. We find them on the political and intellectual plane among those who rediscover their Christian roots since in reaction to the Muslims' presence, and in opposition to it, often through controversies over religious symbols, as is the case in Italy for the crucifix or in France for the *hijiab* (and it is symptomatic of this identity reactivity that these positions are often found, even more vociferous, among declared atheists – think of the Oriana Fallaci case, or Michel Houellebecq, or parties like the 'celtic' North League in Italy – than among believers of other religions). But we find forms of reactive identity also among Muslims who have rediscovered in some way their roots, showing them through specific symbols, opinion and attitudes or the self-segregation in ghetto-like communities) since they have been living in Europe. The same use of a self-definition, on the Muslims' side as well as on 'anti-Muslim' autochthones' side, in terms of "community" is part of this process: as if they were really so, as if there were only *one* community, as if all the members of the supposed community actually belonged to it, or adhered to it, or recognised themselves as part of it. A good example of reactive identities is conflicts on Islamic symbols in Europe.

The presence of Islam inside the European public space could not pass unobserved, either socially or culturally. It is too visible not to lead to debate and tension: a sign that it really is an event that touches sensitive chords, or that is perceived as such.

Islam is disputed in itself, often through essentialistic and simplistic interpretations of the kind of rapport between religion and politics that it proposes. Islam is then disputed in some of its aspects, in how they manifest themselves especially in Muslim countries: of these aspects, the most mediatised are certainly the condition of women and fundamentalism (and related phenomena). Lastly, it leads to debate on the foundations of our societies, on the limits of their possibilities of "openness", on their boundaries, on the many interpretations of possible "tolerance thresholds". All this happens without there often being a direct confrontation/clash with Muslims: often it is a question of internal debates in the host society, *about* Muslims and Islam.

These debates *on* Islam are very wide-ranging, even if what sets them off and their temporal recurrences can be brought down to a limited number of issues. There are however some issues that also imply a social and cultural confrontation/clash which involves Muslim social actors directly (but not necessarily Muslim populations as a whole, as we too readily tend to say), and which have led to discussions, hostilities, forms of refusal or afterthoughts.

The observer has the sensation that the debate that is emerging from these forms of tension has in reality a common theme, and this is what integration is (whatever the word could mean and is appropriate), and how it can be attained: whether the topic in discussion is Islamic schools or the *hijab*, mosques or radical movements, women's rights or forced marriages, and in general anything that creates discussion and tension in the public sphere.

The question of the *hijab* is a typical case. Anyone who has had occasion to hold courses, seminars or conferences on Islam knows how sensitive, how intensely felt, this subject is: almost a point of reference for any discussion on the presence of Islam in the public space, and in general on the question of women in Islam and comparisons between the (supposed) Western and the (supposed) Islamic model, both too easily taken for granted. From a controversy discussed *in* the public space, like that of the *hijab*, we pass to a controversy *about* the public space. Another issue frequently discussed is in fact that of mosques and cemeteries, not simply as such, but perceived as symbolic and central places for making Islam visible.

A point that seems even more crucial implying, as it does, a perception of control of territory, and its symbolic imprinting. An aspect that even with all due caution could be studied not only with the tools of cultural sociology, and sociology *tout court*, but also with the categories proper to ethology and sociobiology. Control of and on territory, after all, is not only a cultural and symbolic fact: it is also (and remains, despite everything) a very concrete and material sign of dominion, of power. Think in particular of the building of mosques, but also simply of the visibility of prayer halls in European cities: questions to which we can add the possibility of spreading the *adhan* outside the mosques, and the building of cemeteries or the granting of specific cemetery spaces. The latter a problem around which the level of hostility is sometimes surprising, considering the fact that granting burial to foreigners is a custom that goes back thousands of years, to be found in all cultures and religions, a fact of human *pietas*, not to mention religious traditions. And considering that, on the other hand, the fact that the immigrant no longer asks for his body to be sent back to the country of origin is, so to speak, a form of *post mortem* integration: the recognition at the very highest symbolic level that the ground in which he wishes to repose for his final sleep he considers his home.

The question of mosques is important for various reasons. On the one hand, in fact, the presence of foreign communities would seem to presuppose as a quite obvious consequence that they would desire to have their own places of religious encounter according to the religion they belong to, as is the case with "internal" autochthonous minorities. But there have been at times surprising conflicts around this question: the sign of discomfort and refusal that is more profound than its specific target in this case. Conflicts that make one think that the question is not the fact in itself (hardly anyone who opposes them would say that they want to stop anyone praying: the reason evoked is always different), but something more profound, connected with symbolic appropriation of territory, which has also something to do with history and its re-construction, but also with deep psychological and social dynamics, to understand which we would perhaps have to venture on to the insidious and slippery ground of cultural psychology. Without forgetting ethology, as I said before. But other subjects are often being discussed: from fundamentalism to multiculturalism, that is, from what we consider unacceptable and impossible to integrate in Islam, to the limits themselves of our capacity for and possibility of welcome.

Islamophobia?

Social processes are never simple. We may at times try to describe them in clear colours, but they actually always appear in *chiaroscuro*. The process at stake is Islam settling in Europe and becoming visible. The topic of discussion, nevertheless, is not the fact in itself, but its manifestations, as they are empirically observable on the ground, or, more often, as they are perceived in the public imaginary, with its pre-judicial (in the literal sense that the judgement is given before the observation) pre-comprehensions, that surround it and in a certain sense anticipate the facts. It is this pre-comprehension that transforms the robes or the beard of a pious traditionalist Muslim into the uniform of an Islamic militant. And this is why the desire to erect mosques as a place of worship and assembly of the community is semantically over-determined, overloaded with meanings that it does not possess, which are connected with fundamentalism and terrorism, or more often with the general fear of a cultural invasion. This is also an example of the "cultural overload" that often affects debates over Islam.

The media play a decisive role both as the expression of a culture – in this case Muslim cultures, in the plural – and as an instrument for reading and interpreting these same cultures, through news of Muslims spread by general and specialised media. They also play a significant even if underestimated role as a means of building Muslim communities and keeping up ties with the countries of origin. Lastly, the media are a sounding box for problems, and constructing criteria for their interpretation.

Public imaginary is crucial. In a certain sense even more than the reality of ongoing social processes, it is from their perception that much of the direction that they take and their success depends. This aspect is of fundamental important also for policies around Islam: which do not so much influence, as *depend* in great measure on the perception of the phenomenon. I will not underline, even though it would be necessary, on the importance of history. I will just limit myself to say that in the case of Islam factors come into play that in the case of other Eastern religions and other cultures do not. I refer in particular to the long past of confrontation/clash with the European West and Christianity, through the Crusades, the long period of maritime conflict against the Saracens and barbarian pirates, but also more recently of colonisation and the complex drift of de-colonization. A story that is not yet over, which also includes the consequences of the Arab-Israel conflict, the Gulf wars, and many local conflicts, from Afghanistan to Iraq, from Lybia to Syria.

"L'Islam vis-à-vis de l'Occident, c'est le chat vis-à-vis du chien", wrote Braudel. And Delumeau, in his history of fear in the West, does not forget the role played by the fear of Islam, traces of which are still to be found not only in history but in the lived reality of folklore (Saracen and Moorgames, among others), in the structure of some Mediterranean cities and landscapes (the Saracen towers that dot the Mediterranean coastlines), in proverbial lore (the Italian "mamma li turchi" – Help! The Turks!): a legacy that it would be ingenuous to think has no effect on the present day. And which weighs at least as much as the Orientalist tradition stigmatised for its defects, with some lack of generosity, by Edward Saïd. The media are unwitting offspring of this mentality, and they take it on board, and in doing so they re-produce it and so make it real, thus turning a legacy from yesterday into a problem of today.

In this complex mechanism of construction of the cultural public imaginary, the media have a central role, which turns out to be more and more determining today, also because their role, following on the processes of globalisation, of which they are at the same time effect, cause and accelerator, is no longer just to inform, but actually to *build* our worlds of knowledge. And to build them not only through the traditional effects of *vertical integration*, inside single nation-states or single societies, or single public spheres, in the words of Habermas, but also by connection and *horizontal integration*, inter-, trans- and super-national (the word integration, incidentally, must not fool us: it is anything but a-conflictual).

Lastly, the world of media visibility is also the world *in which* and *through which* Islam is also seen. And at the same time Muslims are indirectly the means by which Islam is being discovered: something that some seem to have a certain awareness of.

One of the ways of making Islam visible is what happens in exceptional cases, which we may interpret as hermeneutic accidents, a jamming in a certain sense of the interpretative codes, and of the representations of these. Think of the Rushdie case, the question of the headscarf or *hijab* in France and elsewhere, the Danish cartoons affair, and other more local ones. Here I just wish to note their basic logic, which helps to give a *certain* image of Islam (conflictual, for example), which also reverberates through the perception of the phenomenon as a whole, and on to the welcome reserved for the social actors who embody it. Think also of the fate of concepts like *jihad*, that burst into the Western public imaginary as a decisive aspect, at least in the perception of it, of Islam *and therefore* of Muslims, *and therefore* also of Muslims in Europe; an interesting example of generalisation of a local(isable) concept at a global level, and along this path of its assimilation into a perception that is now trans-national. One of its expressions is what is now often termed as Islamophobia.

The rejection of Islam and Islamophobia

The conflicts we have mentioned are obviously the result of the more general climate around Islam and attitudes towards Muslims in Europe: not only, but they are symptoms of extraordinary efficacy. They immediately reveal if we are in a situation of normality and so inside a relatively linear process of integration, or on the contrary if there are important signs at least of suspicion and distrust, if not of real Islamophobia.

The word has a recent and still contested history: even though already present in previous years, it first really became widespread with the report *Islamophobia: A Challenge for Us All*, published by the Runnymede Trust in 1997. A first empirical survey came out in 2002 with the *Summary Report on Islamophobia in the EU after September 11*. A significant form of 'officialization' of the term appeared with the seminar organised at the United Nations on 'Confronting Islamophobia: Education for Tolerance and Understanding' in December, 2004, in which the then Secretary General Kofi Annan participated. Following on this, other agencies joined, among them the Organization of the Islamic Conference (OIC), which set up an observatory on Islamophobia, and since 2008 has been producing monthly bulletins and an annual report on the subject. In these last years various sites have also dedicated themselves to it (among which www.islamophobia.org and www.islamophobia-watch.com), and practically all Islamic information sites, especially European and American, now have a section of documentation dedicated to Islamophobia.

Despite the essential officialization of the term, its use has stirred up much criticism, also in spheres that could certainly never have been suspected of anti-Islamism, even though it has now entered into the language and literature on the Islamic presence at an international level. Islamophobia indeed has a meaning that is not always etymologically correct: what it signals is not necessary *fear* of Islam. It can be something else and even worse: hate that is unmotivated or motivated by other than fear, the expression (one of the many possible) of aggressive drives that do not have their origin in the object on which they work themselves out (so not fear *of Islam*). But it can also be a bland fear, a reasoned preoccupation which can be motivated rationally concerning the evolutions of society, which the word Islamophobia radicalizes and reduces to an extreme kind. This does not obviously mean that Islamophobia does not exist, but that the term used extensively reduces all reactive phenomena to the same kind, as it is not able to grasp differences that are subtle in order and grade, ending up sometimes by constructing the object of analysis instead of defining it correctly. It might be more correct to speak – and it is certainly not less worrying – of the growth of an anti-Muslim climate of feeling in Europe.

In short, Islamophobia seems like a sort of fever, and the conflicts concerning Islam and Muslims an excellent thermometer to measure its level, to see how much the patient is suffering. Now, the fever is never the illness, but a symptom of it, which leads us to inquire into its origins. The only note of optimism in it, is that normally it is a transient phenomenon, which never lasts very long; even though we would not like to say that it has already reached its height today in Europe.

Many reports today enumerate example upon example. If anything the problem is that these long lists constitute only a sum, not yet an explanation. An explanation that can be seen at various levels of complexity. A first level is the simple application to Muslims and their visible presence of the classic 'Nimby' (Not in my back yard) syndrome. More complex, more subtle, more problematic to reflect over a more complex mechanism of 'reactive identities': identities that are created in reaction and in opposition to another identity – whether this other identity is real or, more often, only an imaginary, culturally constructed one (and where the principle, too – the very existence of a certain identity – is under discussion).

Characteristic of such identities are, among others, the over-determination or over-semanticization of cultural elements. A prominent example in Europe today are those who are rediscovering their Christian roots, at a political, cultural, even intellectual level, much more than at the religious one, in opposition to the new arrival of Muslims. But another example, on the other hand, is among those Muslims that, in the West, are discovering or re-discovering (in reality re-inventing) their Islamic roots through forms of closure, self-ghettoization, etc. The mechanism is the same, and testimonies to the fact that it is not attributable to one or the other group as a specific characteristic but if anything it is characteristic of the times and the historical period that we are going through.

Reactive identities produce conflicts, especially conflicts on and about symbols, and particularly religious symbols, because they are well placed to be exploited and used like a flag, around which consensus can be obtained.

Among those who use them with greater efficacy there are those that we could call 'political entrepreneurs of Islamophobia'. The political parties that take Islamophobia as the central part of their programme, and at the same time as an efficient method of gaining consensus, are in strong expansion in most European countries. And they systematically use the conflicts on Islamic issues as a means of visibilization, obtaining notable results on this plane in terms of success. The main problem of their activism in the conflicts – beyond the serious cultural fallout and that on civil cohabitation, to which sooner or later we will have to give a thought – is that they have an evident interest in stoking up the conflict, but none in finding a solution to it. Their political success proceeds and increases as long as the conflict remains open: the moment the conflict is in some way resolved, and the tension and the attention disappear, the political entrepreneurs of Islamophobia lose their centrality, their visibility and their consensus. And it is for this reason that they are the worst enemies of any attempt to find a solution to the conflict: simply they have no interest in doing so. Which makes their role for the whole of society and not only for Muslims particularly problematic: because society, on the contrary, has no interest in protracting the conflicts, which are socially, culturally, politically and also economically, costly, and in the long run produce secondary effects that are strongly negative on the processes of integration and on the actors themselves involved in the conflict. The role of political entrepreneurs of Islamophobia, and the conflict leads to taking sides (and certainly not to listening and seeking the reasons of the adversary), and to an intense activity of legitimation of the reasons of the conflict and of the systematic demonization of the adversary. Finally, this radical form of legitimation of the conflict leads to the use of a language with the adversary (and especially Muslims, wholesale so to speak: not some specific groups or certain individuals) of such roughness that we would refuse to accept it in the case of any other social group: particularly on public occasions and in the public space.

The word Islamophobia has however an unpleasant ring of victimisation to it. While it does refer to social facts that do definitely exist, and which it is important to monitor, its use is particularly seductive for Muslims, putting all the responsibility for its existence on to their host societies. Now, while it is no doubt true that inflammatory anti-Islamic messages have been spreading over Europe, some Islamic leadership, imams and associations bear a non-secondary part of the responsibility for their spreading: for the hypocrisy of some messages or the abstractness of others, for the violence of certain verbal attitudes (occasionally with too weak condemnations from the part of other Muslims) or for the incomprehension of some basic categories and methodologies of common European thinking, for certain extremes of language or defensive lexical hair-splitting, as well as the explicit choice of violence of some people (from Mohamed Atta, who flew into the Twin Towers, to Muhammad Bouyeri, the murderer of Theo Van Gogh, to the suicide bombers operating on European soil – as in Madrid and in London – or, beyond Europe, in the Islamic world, in Palestine as in Casablanca or in Iraq). Obviously they do not concern Muslims in Europe as such, and not even the majority of them; but quite comprehensible they fall over all of them.

Muslims' perception of their religion (in Europe)

Up to now we have mainly analyzed the attitudes towards Islam of the European non-Muslim population. The other side of the coin is at least as much important: the Muslims' perception of their own religion, and how this perception is influenced by the non-Muslim European (Western) perception of Islam.

A first problem is linked to the use of the category Islam in order to talk about and to understand Muslims. This excess of prominence consists in the highlighting of only one – supposed – peculiarity, defined *a priori* (usually in ways that also owe much to an unconsciously Orientalistic approach), with which is explained, or there is an attempt to explain, every possible act and form of behaviour of Muslims – also what could be attributed to other factors. This approach, among other things, tends to accentuate the communitarian dimension of Islam, and often fears (or at times exalts) its irreducible diversity. A good example of this approach may be a certain kind of Orientalism (or worse, its mass media popular version) incapable of distinguishing between the Islam described in books and that lived (or even not lived) by Muslims, who recognise themselves more or less (or *do not* recognise themselves) in it: a form of *essentialism*, which basically proceeds from a predefined image of what Islam is, in which it tries to bodily collocate in flesh and blood those Muslims that find themselves in its path. And if they do not fit, too bad for them... An approach that is not limited to Orientalism. Many of these (theologians, political experts, journalists and sociologists) who, in second-hand works, borrow concepts about the Islam of Muslim countries (majoritarian Islam) and apply them slavishly to the Islam of Europe (minoritarian), and do not grasp their fundamental diversity, are carrying out precisely this sort of essentialistic operation.

Essentialism, the search for "what a thing cannot but be", which in other fields can led to fertile developments, runs the risk of being quite misleading in sociology (specifically in the sociology of Islam), even if it responds to some characteristics that make it attractive as a method from the point of view of the scholar: it is relatively easy to study, it has an undoubted didactic efficacy, it gives the illusion of immediate comprehension and thus satisfies any anxieties as to interpretation, it adapts very well to academic rituals (cultured citations, footnotes, attachment to a tradition, ritual homage to past masters, etc.), and it also woks very well in a mediatic logic.It also has debatable results in the kind of "reflexivity" it produces on society, leading to a pre- interpretation in cultural and religious terms that is both scientifically and politically problematic in its consequences.

What it is important to note here is that this essentialistic approach to Islam is typical also of the Islamic discourses proposed and 'acted' in the public space by many Muslim representatives and organisations in Europe: it can be commonly found in speeches, articles, books, websites, press releases and declarations, etc. But if this kind of approach can be understandable inside the precinct of strict religious discourses, as in qutbas, for instance (it is not different, by the way, from the discourses one can find in other religious - but also political - communities), its complete lack of empirical bases and its tendency to excessive generalisation is heavily problematic in order to understand socio-religious behaviours, beliefs and belongings of religious people. It can be a propagandistic tool (but not necessarily an useful and well working one), but it is an educational gigantic fault and an analytical disaster: and when Muslims want to act collectively in order to obtain results (in short, if they want to act politically) or when they simply present themselves in the public sphere, or even worse when they want to form and educate militants and supporters of groups and organizations, this way of thinking and of approaching concepts creates more problems than it solves through its apparent simplicity, which is after all just a misleading simplicism.

"Meccan and "ummic": on minority Islam

One of the elements of deep dissatisfaction towards this approach is that it systematically underestimates the specificity of the fact that European Islam is an Islam in a minority situation. Thus, it cannot be equated with the Islam defined as *din, dunya wa dawla*, which is religion, everyday life (literally, the low temporal existence, earthly life) and organized living, i.e. institutional, government in its modern form, state, and hence politics. On the other hand, this image, which is often used to interpret majority Islam, is probably a mere intellectual construct. It is also interesting to note that the Arabic root of the word *dawla*, which is used to indicate a reign or dynasty, and by extension a power, also means alternation, change, and instability, almost as though to underline the inevitable transient dimension of any political and institutional structure. Incidentally, this also applies to religious structure in that no legitimizing centre exists that is able to issue licences of orthodoxy or heterodoxy, and this dimension is therefore substantially subject to the logic of *de facto* powers of contractualization and contestation, but also permanent regeneration. The imbalance is experienced in a very modern way as largely structural. And if this is true for majority and hence hegemonic Islam, it is all the more true for minority Islam.

Nevertheless much cultural production *on* Islam and much production that comes to us *from* Islam implicitly considers Islam as a majority religion. It could not be otherwise: Islam defines itself as such, even theologically – hence the importance of constructing a minority theology starting from the European situation which authors like Tariq Ramadan and organizations like the European Council for Fatwa and Research in London are attempting to do. It is no coincidence that Islam instituted its calendar at Yathrib-Medina at precisely the moment in which it became a majority religion; this shift from Mecca to Medina, in the *hijra* of 622 AD was its date of birth. Islam was not born with the birth of the Prophet, but with the community founded by him. By transferring from Mecca to Medina, Islam itself changed from being a minority religion, a marginal sect in contemporary terms, to become a majority one and, therefore, law and government – a state church in modern sociological terms. And Muhammad, from being the *guru* of a movement of religious revival which tended to seek its followers at the lower rather than higher end of the social stratification at Mecca, became on a larger scale what he was only for his few followers: prophet and envoy of God, religious authority, but also, that it was more decisive for the evolution of Islam as we know it in the political, legislative, juridical spheres and even military authority. It was at Medina, and only here, that the Muslim *umma* was truly born in the historic sense that gave it its character and identity.

The irony of fate is that present-day European Islam finds itself in a situation that is far more similar to that which prevailed in Mecca than Medina, i.e. it is a tolerated minority religion that is sometimes stigmatized and sometimes integrated and institutionalized, but it remains a minority religion. Moreover, being a minority religion has important sociological consequences.

Not only is European Islam "Meccan", it is also "ummic". In the history of Islam, starting from the Arabian Peninsula where it was born, expansion has always originated in some kind of ethnic drive, even if the ethnic groups leading Islamic supremacy and the responsibility for its spreading have changed: from the original Arab combatants (plural in their internal relations), to Persians, Turks, Mongols, or many others who took into their hands – not only metaphorically – the sword of Islam. This characteristic of internal plurality is far more accentuated in present-day Europe. The origins of Muslims are multiple, and even in those countries in which there is an identifiable ethnic group or dominant geographical provenance among Muslim immigrants (e.g. Turks in Germany, Indo-pakistanis in United Kingdom, Maghrebians in France), in reality it is difficult to identify it, or it is becoming less and less identifiable: there is no single origin nor an original centre of power that is easily identifiable.

Turks in Germany, for instance, while having the same national origin, divide their religious references and obediences between those who identify with official gov-ernmental Diyanet Islam, those who refer to movements such as IGMG, but there are also Alevis, Kurds, Kaplang-is, etc. So, despite the fact of being all Turks (and some of them, in the second generations, are no longer Turks by nationality, but only Germans, or bear both nationalities), they differ significantly (and sometimes conflict each oth-er) on other terms.

Instead, the observable panorama shows not only a plurality of presences and contributions in terms of law schools (all co-existing which makes them lose much of their traditional meaning) and mystical confraternities (a far greater diversity of which can be encountered in the West than elsewhere and whose boundaries are easier to cross in Europe), but also a plurality of ethnic groups (Ar-abs, Turks, Indopakistanis, Black Africans, etc., with all their internal divisions), a plurality of "religious families" (Sunnites of all kinds, Shiites, etc.). Finally, it also shows a plurality of languages both those of the countries of origin which are numerous (first and foremost Arabic, Turkish, Persian, Urdu, Wolof, and many others) and the European languages, the dominant languages in this respective the host countries. The latter are often the only languages in which all immigrants of Muslim origin can communicate among themselves. This becomes even more applicable the further removed they are from the moment of immigration and is increasingly the case as the first generation of im-migrants is replaced by the second, third etc., no longer definable as such.

In many ways, the *umma* – in its complexity and plurality – is far more visible in Europe than in the countries of origin where believers can only find other persons like themselves, of the same nationality, language, belief, and interpretation of these beliefs (within a specific law school). Only on the occasion of the *hajj* (and in this case, of course, to a greater extent – but temporarily) can a Muslim experience the *umma* as a concrete and visible reality and not only as a symbolic one in the same vivid way that the common believer can usually, on a daily life basis we might say, experience it in many mosques and Islamic organizations in Europe. The internal diversity among Muslims is more evident in Europe, the USA, and in other countries of migration than elsewhere, and certainly more than in the countries of origin of these immigrants. And this internal diversity has important consequences. A particularly relevant example is provided by the law schools which are so crucial for the self-interpretation of Islam. All of the *madhhab* in Europe are "living"; but the major difference from the situation in the countries of origin is that they mix much more easily, and individuals can find their way *through* them even more than *in* one of them. To use the words of one of my interviewees, born in Africa but of Yemeni origin and living in London: "I am *shafii*, but I have to follow the most common *madhab* here which is the *hanafi* one. Personally, as far as the *hajj* is concerned I am *hanafi*, for *jihad* I am *maliki*, for the conception of minority I am *hanbali*...". Thus it is no coincidence that European Muslims are beginning to speak of the European school – the Western and minority one (including the United States) – as of the "fifth law school" under construction.

Islam in Europe: stages of proximity

We have delineated up to now the clearly different new situation in which Islam in Europe is situated, compared to that of the countries of origin. But it must also be said that the countries of origin, and their Islam, become less a reference for Europeans Muslims, the more time and generation passes. From this point of view we can describe the links between Islam and Europe in terms of changing stages of proximity. During a prolonged *first stage*, *Islam and (Christian) Europe*, which were conceived and saw themselves as mutually impermeable and self-centred, stood in opposition to each other despite reality and history which show how the permeability of philosophical ideas, scientific notions, artistic – and also economic and commercial – forms and exchange were more the norm than the exception.

During the *second stage*, it was Europe that penetrated far into the lands and culture of Islam in the age of Empires and the period of colonization and then in contemporaneous neo-colonization, which passed through the processes of both economic and symbolic globalization, and that of consumerism, media etc. Thus, here we see a penetration by *Europe into Islam*. The *third stage*, which is more recent (in some countries, like France, it had already begun in the period between the two world wars, but in most cases it started from the post-war years of reconstruction and then following on the economic boom of the 1950s and 1960s in central-northern Europe, and even later, from the end of the 1970s onward, in southern Europe), marks the start of the presence of *Islam in Europe* through migration. During a *fourth stage* we see the birth and consolidation of an *Islam of Europe* as a result of the progression through generations and a more general cultural change which took place primarily at a personal level. The natural follow-on of this process should be a *fifth stage*, of which we can now only see the uncertain beginnings, involving the formation of a real *European Islam* with a proper and marked identity which differs to that of Arabian Islam, for example. When referring to this Islam we should speak of European citizens of Muslim origin or of Islamic culture and/or religion instead of Muslims living in Europe. Even if it is possible to detect signs of the onset of this fifth stage, most countries of Europe today are, with the majority of their Muslim populations, somewhere between the third and fourth stages.

Problems and contradictions in contents, visibility and action

One of the problems of reciprocal comprehension that Muslims in Europe and European non- Muslims do have, is that often they both do not perceive the importance of these changes of phase, and because of this they perpetuate a conflictual dicotomical image (Europe/Islam, in worst cases Europe vs. Islam or Islam vs. Europe) that does not correspond to the evolutions we have tried to describe. The two interlocutors often talk of each other (and of themselves) as if they were still in the first stage. What must be observed as a movie in which the (social) actors pass through experiences that mark their evolution and growth, is still described, too often, in terms of a set of pictures taken in the past and/or in the countries of origin – a misunderstanding which is terribly rich in terms of its (negative) consequences: among other things in the way Islam (and Islam in Europe) is perceived.

We have no time and possibility to understand these negative consequences in detail. I will limit myself, in the following lines, to enumerate some of the main problems observable on the Muslims' side of the question, both in the reality of Muslims' social life and in the way Muslims often present and re-present themselves in the public sphere.

At the social level, one of the critical elements concerns family life and family problems, included gender issues, to be understood between male and female parents and, even more critical, between parents and their sons and, particularly, daughters. Obviously, not only Muslims, and possibly not mainly Muslims, have problems in this realm. Equally obvious, there are a lot of positivities Muslims might try to refer to. But it is interesting to note how far the incomprehension has gone. As the director of an important Islamic Centre said to me: "We have to show Europeans how beautiful the Islamic model (of gender division and family roles) is. How it happens that you don't see that?" Well, simply compare this statement (made by an honest covered polygamous representative) with the average image of Muslim families, parents and, particularly, fathers in European public discourses in media, politics, religion... It is undoubtedly true that this argument has become a polemic tool, often offensive and frequently instrumentalised for conflictual purposes, from the part of journalists, intellectuals, politicians, etc. But can it be only this? In this sense, the lack of self-criticism, the difficulty in elaborating discourses capable to take into account the objections (all unfounded?) of European non-Muslims (not necessarily anti-Muslims) is, at this stage, dramatic. Another problematic issue concerns the high percentage of presence of Muslim origin people in prisons, or involved in forms of illegal activities, in some form of social and individual violence, etc. It is absolutely true that this has usually nothing to do with religion in itself, and that many of these people are not particularly religious, and that in any case is not their religion responsible for their acts – we are talking, after all, of social problems. But can Muslims in Europe limit themselves to these considerations, even if correct? Or should they act more, considering this at least a defeat for their capacity to maintain an acceptable degree of identification with religious principles in significant percentages of their population and, particularly, youth? Something should be dealt with, and not left to volunteers and solidarity NGOs' (often of another religion).

At the intellectual and mediatic level much can be done. Quickly abandoning the structural reaction (the self reflection) in terms of victimization might be an excellent way to confront the image of Islam and Muslims in the public space in a productive way. Producing an Islamic press more capable of criticism and self criticism, using new languages different from traditional paternalism could be very important. Some sense of humour might help in reaching this objective.

Quite obviously, the diffusion at all levels of salafi and neo-salafi imported discourses must be seen as a critical element, from this point of view. As much as the experimentation of new languages in the web, in media like TV and satellite channels, radio, etc., goes positively in the opposite direction. By the way, the use of English or of the languages of the country of emigration is part, and a significant one, of this positive indirect answer to neo-salafi literature and attitudes. At the religious level, much must be said. But much also should be done. Among others, concerning the popular diffusion of anti-Jews opinions and prejudices, and less frequently of anti-Christian statements (e.g. defining them, internally, as *kafirun*, an expression much different from that of *dhimmi* or of *ahl al- kitab*, used in dialogical contexts). Of course, this language is peculiar and parallel to the demonisation of Islam we have already talked about. But should we all continue this way, in this measure?

At the political level much should be said. But a serene discussion on political and religious violence (Islamic terrorism included) is still yet to come. And some evolutions are expected, also comparing to the season of internal political terrorism many European states have passed through, and how this season has been passed over.

Conclusion: on conflict and change

As we have seen, conflict can be read in many different ways. Sociologically, conflict has a positive function. Furthermore, as the classics of sociology have taught us, from Marx to Weber and Simmel, cannot be eliminated. As Heraclitus said: "It is necessary to know that justice is conflict". After all, crisis prompts the discussion of a problem

– always too late, but always better late than never. Crisis and conflict also help us to discover how far we can go and which social boundaries cannot be exceeded. Leadership is forged in conflict. In conflict we have to ask ourselves about a sense of common responsibility which must not produce harmful excesses that may rebound on those who produce them: we measure our real strength, but also that of others, and that of society, its rules, its tools for regulation. Through conflict we test who we are, but also who others are and the idea of otherness. In conflict situations we learn to measure the difference between what we are, what we want, and what we can obtain. Moreover, conflict is a means of bringing to the surface of consciousness what lies and bubbles in the depths. Taking opinions to extremes has after all a function, which is precisely this: to make visible what is not usually visible, make the unconscious conscious, the unaware aware, and letting words say what is not usually said.

As is the case with couples and families, the healthy ones are not those that do not experience conflict, but those in which conflict finds channels to emerge, be dealt with, and resolved. When this does not happen, families break up, or their members continue to live together in a state of constant unhappiness. This is not a good solution or one to be desired. As happens in democracy, which after all is a method not for avoiding conflict, but facing it without recourse to violence, instead of killing my adversary, I vote. As happens in the case of social conflict, for example, in the workplace, i.e. conflict arises and is inevitable, but can be dealt with through a revolution or a strike.

Society *is* conflictual by definition. In a real sense, conflict is the only way we have to avoid war. By taking it into consideration and managing it, we manage to avoid any explosion of violence. However, if we have learnt to regulate political conflict (representative democracy) and social conflict (industrial relations), we have not yet found

a stable system for regulating cultural and religious conflict that is accepted by all. It is no coincidence that today
the preachers of conflict and of cultural clash are enjoy-
ing great success on different sides. This is the reason why
what could be a physiology of social conflict, developed in a
cultural form, risks becoming a pathology: it is always like
that when, and as long as, those who gain from conflict are
in greater numbers or simply play their cards better than
those who do not want conflict to be overcome (because
that is not possible) but simply regulated and made to lower its tone a little. Moreover, there will always be people
who have an interest in fomenting or even creating and
"inventing" conflict where it doesnot exist or could be diminished, solved, or dealt with.

From this point of view, the danger we face is great:
the clash of civilizations – not only on a planetary scale, but
also in our cities and neighbourhoods – is not at play, but it
may be a self- fulfilling prophecy. It is by dint of repeating
it, recalling it, invoking it, that we produce it and we make it
real. In a certain sense it is a trench that we are digging for
ourselves with our own hands. Furthermore the conflict is
not only, and perhaps not mainly, *between* cultures and religions or better, more accurately, between their representatives: it is *internal* to cultures, religions, and communities.
Today, society is divided on different questions to those on
which it was divided in the past. With the decline of class
distinctions (at least in the common ideological interpretations and intellectual and media opinions, albeit less in
reality), we are increasingly divided today over factors of in-
clusion and exclusion that are often very material (expens-
es, interests, costs and benefits, taxes, services), but equally
often cloaked in ethnic, racial, cultural, or pseudo-cultural
and religious justifications.

Diversity, or otherness, is becoming a problem or
even a flaw in itself. This means that other social actors (including religious ones) are also being divided increasingly

not only and not so much among themselves, but within themselves, i.e. between those who engage in dialogue and those who do not, those who are open to change and those who are not, those ready to put themselves on the line and/or put society on the line and those who do not even consider this (also in the face of the facts and changes that have *already* taken place which they do not even wish to consider), and between those who are hence ready to measure up to diversity and otherness and those who deny their very bases. These positions are, of course, complemented by all manner of conceivable intermediate attitudes.

On the other hand, precisely because, for the reasons set out above, conflict is necessary, constitutive of society, physiological, and inevitable (in particular in the presence of such significant changes and the fact that Islam is today the second largest religion in Europe cannot be considered a detail of history), we can hypothesize that in its present form with its extensive radicalization and visibility it is only one inevitable stage, even if this stage is unlikely to be short(or perhaps has yet to peak), that is unfolding while we wait to find forms of regulation more suited to the conflict itself. In this sense we can try to be optimistic or have some reasonable hope of emerging from the crisis. A new level of equilibrium may be born. This may be a new society, for which we do not (yet) have any plans and rules, but which we are trying to construct. This may be indicated by the long-term trends we are seeing within the Islamic communities of Europe – tendencies that could generally be referred to as the Europeanization of Islam, i.e. the adaptation of its cultural and normative framework (a Europeanization that ranges from gender relations to theological changes, from forms of family and cultural integration to economic integration and consumer models).

Islam in Europe is changing. However, in the process of making itself European, by becoming a European reality and an internal social actor, it is also changing Europe.

Furthermore, through personal links and organized net-works as well as the old and new media, the Muslims who live in what we could call the European part of the *umma* also influence their Islamic areas of origin, including those from which first generations of immigrants originated, through numerous feedback effects. In the same way, due to the mere existence of the Islamic presence, Europe is changing. To mention just one example, this is visible on the micro-level simply in the different attitude that teachers of religion are forced to adopt if they have pupils of different religions, or none at all, in their classes (the example can be extended to an infinite number of potential situations and social roles, most obviously to the case of mixed couples and families), despite the fact that they may or may not be prepared for this change or may or may not be subjectively open to it. The simple fact of being physically confronted with "the other" forces them to think more profoundly. On the macro- level, this change is visible in politics and poli-cies about the legal regulation of religion in thepublic space and, more practically, in the everyday functioning of social services and reform of school programmes.

So, as I have noted elsewhere, from now on it will not be possible to understand the history and the social and re-ligious evolution of Europe without taking its Islamic com-ponent into account. In the same way, it will not be possible to understand the history, social and theological evolution of Islam without taking into account its European compo-nent. The history of Europe has become an Islamic histo-ry – at least in part – and the history of Islam has become European history. It is up to you, to me, to us, to make it a reality as peaceful as possible.

There are many good things happening. But I have been invited to talk about problems. This does not mean that there are no solutions for them. They can, they must be found. It is your effort. Mine, in this occasion, is just analytical. Yours is much more than this: it is existential. So, good luck...

Bibliographical note

I have focused on the topics raised in this paper in several articles and books. Among the articles, see at least, on the construction of the Muslim image, my *How the Immigrant has become Muslim. Public Debates on Islam in Europe*, in "Revue Européenne des Migrations Internationales", vol. 21, n. 2, 2005, pp.135-161; on conflicts see *Konflikte um islamische Symbole in Europa*, in "Journal fur Konflikt- und Gewaltforschung", n. 2, 2003, pp.6-32, and *Conflicts, Cultures and Religions: Islam in Europe as a Sign and Symbol of Change in European Societies*, in "Yearbook on Sociology of Islam", n.3, 2005, pp.18-27. Among the books, see in particular, for a general assessment, *Muslims in the Enlarged Europe* (eds. B.Maréchal, S.Allievi, F.Dassetto, J.Nielsen), Leiden-Boston, Brill, 2003. On the role of networks see *Muslim Networks and Transnational Communities in and across Europe* (eds. S.Allievi and J.Nielsen), Leiden-Boston, Brill, 2003. On mosques and mosque conflicts see the final report of the largest European comparative research on this issue *Conflicts over Mosques in Europe. Policy issues and trends*, London, Alliance Publishing Trust / Network of European Foundations, 2009; see my introduction and all the national reports in *Mosques of Europe. Why a solution has become a problem* (ed. S.Allievi), London, Alliance Publishing Trust / Network of European foundations, 2010 (both are accessible with free download from my website www.stefanoallievi.it).On the crucial theme of production of religious knowledge see *Producing Islamic Knowledge. Transmission and dissemination in Western Europe* (eds. M.Van Bruinessen and S.Allievi), London-New York, Routledge, 2011 also translated in Turkish as *Avrupa'da Müslüman Öznenin Üretimi: Fikirler, Bilinçler, Örnekler*, İstanbul, İletişim, 2012.

Müzakere

Doç. Dr. Kadir Canatan (Türkei)

Teşekkürler sayın başkan.

Şimdi sayın Allievi'nin başlığından hareketle, konuşmasını iki eksen üzerinde yürüttüğünü gördük. Birinci bölümde, kamusal alanda, Avrupa'da İslam hakkında yapılan tartışmalara değindi. İkinci bölümde de bu tartışmaların Müslümanlara etkisi nedir, özellikle İslam'ı algılama biçimlerine, kimliklerine etkisi nedir, bu konuyu tartışmaya çalıştı. Oldukça sistematik bir analiz yaptı. Daha çok mevcut durumu tasvir etmeye yöneldi. Olması gerekeni söylemekten ziyade, olan nedir, olanı anlamaya çalışalım dedi bize, bir anlamda. Ve İslam'ın Avrupa'daki gelişimini belirli aşamalar hâlinde ele almamızı söyledi. Bu bağlamda beş aşamadan bahsetti, ben bunları tekrarlamayacağım. Fakat bizi ilgilendiren özellikle son üç aşama, yani 1960'tan bu yana meydana gelen gelişmeler. 60'lı yıllarda Müslüman ülkelerden Avrupa'ya yönelik göç temelinde, Avrupa'da bir İslam varlığı ortaya çıkmaya başladı. Bunu üçüncü aşama olarak görüyor, daha öncesinde de iki aşama olduğunu söyledi. Dördüncü aşama ise İslam'ın burada yerleşmesi ve kurumsallaşması. Çünkü birinci dönemde, yani 60'lı ve 70'li yıllarda Müslümanların geçici olduğu varsayılıyordu. 80'den sonra bu düşünce bir tarafa itildi ve Müslümanların burada kalıcı olduğu tezi resmî olarak kabul edilmeye başlandı. Bu andan itibaren de İslam'ın kurumsallaşması süreci yaşandı. Bu bizi nereye getirdi? Bugün durduğumuz noktayı, kendisinin deyimiyle beşinci aşamayı Avrupa İslamı'nın ortaya çıkışı şeklinde tanımlıyor.

Aslında burada iki süreç var; bir tarafta İslam'ın burada yerleşmesi ve kurumsallaşmasıyla, Avrupa'nın İslamlaşması diyebileceğimiz bir süreç var, öte taraftan da İslam'ın burada kurumsallaşması sürecinin İslam'ı yeniden yorumlamaya yönelik bir boyutu var. Bu da İslam'ın Avrupalılaşması sürecini beraberinde getiriyor. Dolayısıyla biz bugün iki süreci birlikte yaşıyoruz. Tabii bu süreç çok doğal, normal bir süreç değil. Çünkü bu süreç içinde karşılıklı olarak birtakım korkular ortaya çıktı. Yani Avrupa "Acaba İslamlaşıyor muyuz?" diye sorarken, İslam'ı bir tehdit olarak algılamaya başlarken, Müslümanlarda da tersine bir başka korku ortaya çıktı: Asimilasyon korkusu. Acaba kendi kimliğimizden, kültürümüzden, dinimizden uzaklaşıyor muyuz? Dolayısıyla her iki tarafta da yaşanan korkular var. Bu korkuların ben kaostan kaynaklandığı kanaatindeyim. Dolayısıyla bugünkü sempozyumun da temel kavramlarından biriydi bu kaos kelimesi.

Kaos mevcut durumun tanımlanamaması demek aslında. Hem Avrupalılar için yeni gelişmeler, değişmeler söz konusu; onlar bunu anlamaya, tanımlamaya çalışıyor. Bu kolay bir şey değil. Hem de Müslümanlar, içinde bulundukları yeni ortamı kendi kimliklerinden, kendi geleneklerinden hareketle anlamaya ve yorumlamaya çalışıyor. Dolayısıyla bu kaostan kurtulmamızın en önemli çıkış yolu, bu tanımlama sürecinin çok sağlıklı bir şekilde gerçekleştirilmesi. Yani içinde bulunduğumuz durumu kabul edilebilir bir düzeyde tanımlamamız gerekiyor.

Ne yazık ki ben daha fazlasını bekliyordum; sayın Allievi İslam'ın Avrupalılaşması bağlamında ileri sürülen görüşleri bildirmedi. Bu kavramı normatif bir anlamda kullanmadığını biliyorum. Ancak en azından mevcut trendler, olası senaryolar üzerinde durulabilirdi. Bize bir yol haritası çizebilirdi bu noktada. Fakat bunu yapmadı, daha çok bugünkü kaosun tepkisel kimliklere yol açtığını söyledi. Bu bence önemli bir kavram. Tepkisel kimlikler sadece Avrupa'da oluşmuyor. Yani bugün Avrupa çok önemli oranda sekülerleşmiş bir Avrupa'dır. Buna rağmen, bakıyorsunuz, Müslümanlar üzerinde yapılan tartışmalarla Avrupa kendi kültürel kökenlerine de bir dönüş hareketi yaşıyor. Yani Avrupa bir anlamda kendini yeniden tanımlamaya başlıyor. Aslında bu süreç göçmenlerde de söz konusu. Yani göçmenler de kendi kültürlerine, kendi kültürel kökenlerine bir dönüş çabası içindeler. Ben bunun sadece kültürel, entelektüel bir çaba olduğunu düşünmüyorum. Özellikle 2000'li yıllarda buna eşlik eden sosyal birtakım gelişmeler var. Mesela dikkat çekicidir, Utrecht Üniversitesi ve Erasmus Üniversitesi'nde iki öğrenci bu konuda master tezi yaptılar; tezlerinde yüksek eğitimli Türk gençlerinin, Türkiye'ye dönüş yaptıklarını, bu yönde güçlü bir eğilimin ortaya çıktığını söylüyorlar. Dolayısıyla kökenlere dönüş sadece kültürel anlamda olmuyor. Bir anlamda hiç beklemediğimiz bir şekilde, birinci kuşağa özgü olarak düşündüğümüz bu geri dönüş düşüncesinin, yeni kuşaklarda da su yüzüne çıktığını görüyoruz. Ve bugün birçok genç burada doğduğu hâlde, Almanya'da çok iyi bir eğitim aldığı hâlde Tükiye'ye dönüyor. Bu konudaki rakamlara ben biraz baktım; son iki yıldır Türkiye'de, bu konularda acaba Türk basını ne yazıyor, çiziyor diye bakıyorum. Doğrusu Türk basınının bu konudan hiç haberi yok, bu konuda haber çıkmadı. Mesela Almanya'da son üç-beş yıl içerisindeki rakamlara baktığımız zaman, her yıl 50.000 Türk, Türkiye'ye dönüyor. Bundan haberiniz var mı? Bir de Hollanda'daki rakamlara baktığımız zaman, son üç-beş yıl içinde, yine ortalama olarak 4000 ila 5000 civarında Türk kendi ülkesine dönüyor. Bunların çok önemli bir kısmı da ikinci kuşak gençlerden oluşuyor. Demek ki kültürel kökenlere dönüş bir anlamda kendi ülkesine dönüş anlamını da içeren bir kavram. Böyle bir sosyal olgu da var.

Bu neden gerçekleşiyor? Bunu çok iyi analiz etmemiz gerekiyor. Ben bir gün Türkiye'ye gidiyordum. Uçakta yanıma bir genç oturdu. Hollanda'da küçük bir şehirde doğup büyümüş. O günlerde o şehirde bir Türk camisi kundaklandı. Bu konu üzerinde konuşurken gencin de, tıpkı benim gibi Türkiye'ye geri dönüş hazırlığı içinde olduğunu gördüm. Piyasa araştırması yapmak üzere Türkiye'ye gidiyormuş. Ben Hollanda'da doğmadım, Türkiye doğumluyum. Lise sona kadar Türkiye'de kaldım, ondan sonra yurt dışına çıktım. Benim geri dönüş eğiliminde olmam bir açıdan anlaşılabilir ama bu genç orada doğmuş, orada büyümüş. Buna rağmen orada kendisine bir gelecek görmüyor. Bunun için Türkiye'de iş araştırması yapmak üzere Türkiye'ye gidiyor. Demek ki burada yapılan tartışmalar, Müslümanlara yönelik saldırılar öyle bir düzeye çıktı ki, 2000'li yıllarda, artık insanlar Türkiye'ye doğru bir geri dönüş eğilimine de girmiş bulunuyorlar. Bu ciddi bir gelişme, çünkü Hollanda'da artık şöyle düşünülüyor: Bizim İslam hakkında yaptığımız tartışmalar ters tepki yarattı, bunlar kendi kimliklerine daha fazla sarılıyorlar, hâlbuki biz bunları Avrupalılaştırmak istiyorduk. Üstelik kendi ülkelerine de kaçmaya başladılar, oysa biz bunlara, bu gençlere yatırım yapmıştık, yüksek eğitim vermiştik, dolayısıyla bu beyin gücünü kaybediyoruz, diye korkuya kapıldılar.

Bu sosyal olaya değindikten sonra ben hızlı bir şekilde esas konuya gelmek istiyorum. Bir kere İslam'ın Avrupalılaşması fikri ne içeriyor? Bu konuda çok net bir tanıma ulaşmazsak, bence bu sürecin sorun yaratacağı kanaatindeyim. Bunun içeriği ve yönü konusunda sosyolojik araştırmalara ihtiyaç var. Her şeyden önce olayın sosyolojik boyutu ile teolojik boyutu arasında bir ayrım yapmamız gerekiyor. Sosyolojik boyut bence teolojik boyutun daha ilerisinde yürüyor bugün. Mesela 2000 yılında, Rotterdam'da Türk, Faslı ve Hollandalı gençler arasında yapılmış bir araştırma var. Burada gençlerin dine ve siyasete yaklaşımları araştırıldı. İlginç sonuçlar ortaya çıktı. Birkaç sonucu aktarmak istiyorum. Mesela Müslüman gençlere, Faslı ve Türk gençlere şu soru yöneltiliyor: İslam ve siyaset ilişkisi konusunda ne düşünüyorsunuz? Genelde üç tane önerme ifade veriliyor, bunlara cevap verilmesi isteniyor. Birinci önerme şu;

İslam'ın siyasetle bir alakası yoktur, din sadece Tanrı ve kul arasındaki bir ilişkidir. Bu ifadeye destek veren, evet diyen Türk ve Faslı gençlerin oranı %65. Yani aslında siyasal olmayan, bir anlamda laik diyebileceğimiz bir görüşü temsil ediyor bu gençler. İkinci bir grup, %30'luk bir grup. Bunlar diyorlar ki, İslam mevcut görüşler içinde, farklı siyasal görüşler içinde bir görüş olabilir. Yani nasıl Avrupa'da Hristiyan Demokratlar varsa, İslam da, Müslüman Demokratlar gibi bir parti şeklinde de siyasallaşabilir. Dikkat edilirse burada gençler mevcut düzeni reddetmeden, çoğulcu sistem içerisinde İslam'ın siyasallaşabileceğini ve bundan da korkulmaması gerektiğini vurguluyorlar. Dolayısıyla çoğulcu bir görüşe sahipler. Şimdi fundamentalistlerine kadar, siyaseti sadece din belirlemelidir görüşüne destek veren Türk ve Faslı gençlerin oranı %2,5'u geçmiyor.

Bu araştırma ne için yapıldı biliyor musunuz? Daha önce Heitmeyer'in Berlin'de yaptığı bir araştırma var. Bu araştırma yayımlandıktan sonra Hollanda'da bir korku oluştu. Çünkü gençlerin İslam devleti istediği yönünde bir sonuç çıkmıştı Heitmeyer'in araştırmasında. Hollanda'da bazı kişiler bundan korktular, acaba bizde durum nasıl oluyor diye. O yüzden böyle bir araştırmayı finanse etmişlerdi. Bir gazete de buna destek vermişti. Burada daha ilginç bir sonuç çıktı: Hollandalı gençlere aynı sorular sorulduğunda, mesela Hollandalı gençlerin %4'ü siyasette din belirleyici olmalıdır görüşüne destek veriyor. Yani eğer fundamentalizm Müslüman gençler arasında bir sorunsa, bu sorun daha fazla Hristiyan gençler arasında bir sorun olarak karşımıza çıktı.

Dolayısıyla bu sonuçları değerlendirdiğim zaman, şöyle bir yorum yapabiliriz: Bence ana eğilimler hâlâ modernleşme süreçleri, trendleri dediğimiz doğrultuda gerçekleşiyor. Yani gençler siyasetten kopuk bir İslam anlayışına sahipler, siyasal İslam'a çok fazla destek yok. Siyasal İslam'a destek verenler de bunun çoğulcu bir sistem içinde olmasını öngörüyorlar. Ve fundamentalizm ciddi bir tehlike değil gençlerimiz arasında. Ben bunu Avrupai İslam yönünde bir gelişme olduğu şeklinde yorumluyorum. Yani Avrupai İslam dediğim modernleşme trendleriyle uyumlu büyüyen bir İslam.

Peki teolojik noktada gelişmeler nedir dersiniz? Maalesef İslam teolojisini yapanlar, üretenler büyük oranda ilahiyatçılar ve imamlar olduğu için, bunlar Türkiye'den, Fas'tan ve diğer Arap ülkelerinden geldikleri için, çok fazla da burada kalmayıp geri döndükleri için, ilahiyat alanında ciddi anlamda bir çalışma olduğu söylenemez. Ama buna rağmen, bakıyorsunuz, birçok kişi artık şu kavramı kabul ediyor: Biz Avrupa'da, Amerika'da azınlık konumundayız, dolayısıyla bir azınlık fıkhından söz edebiliriz. Çünkü geleneksel fıkıh ekolleri Müslümanların çoğunlukta olduğu toplumlarda gelişti ve Müslümanların azınlık konumlarına dikkat çekmiyor, onu hesaba katmıyor.

Bir arkadaşım, Amsterdam Frey Üniversitesi'nde imamlar üzerinde bir araştırma yapıyor. O gitmiş Diyanet'e sormuş; Avrupa'dan gelen sorular oluyor mu, bunlara nasıl cevap veriyorsunuz, diye. Ve bu soruları geldiği ülkelere göre tasnif ettiniz mi, şeklinde sorular soruyor. Maalesef, onlar diyorlar ki; soru nereden gelirse gelsin bizim için soruya verilecek cevaplar her zaman aynıdır. Yani Avrupa'da sorulmuş bir soruyla, söz gelimi Türkiye'de veya bir Arap ülkesinde sorulmuş bir soru onlar için çok farklı anlamlar içermiyor. Bu şunu gösteriyor: Mevcut dinî kurumlar, ilahiyatçılar henüz Avrupa ortamını, Avrupa'daki özel şartları çok fazla dikkate almıyorlar. Dolayısıyla ben bu sosyolojik gelişmeyle teolojinin, fıkhın bir anlamda arasının zamanla açılacağını düşünüyorum. Ve esas problem de bence o zaman başlayacak. Onun için, Avrupa İslamı'nın sadece sosyolojik bir fenomen olmadığını, teolojik bir boyutu da olması gerektiğini bir an önce düşünmemiz ve bu konuda çabalamamız gerekiyor, diye düşünüyorum.

Çok teşekkür ederim.

Universal Islam or Euro-Islam: The Politics of a European Islam

Dr. S. Sayyid (England)

Introduction

Bassam Tibi quotes with approval an article in *Time* magazine in which he was cited as stating that there is no "middle way between Euro-Islam and a ghettoization of Muslim minorities" (Tibi 2009:143). Tibi's rendering of his argument sits uncomfortably with his claim that "polarization is alien" to him, since his entire thesis is based on a polarization between the Islamization of Europe and the Europeanization of Islam (ibid.:128, 129). Tibi illustrates once again how various points in history 'Muslim' and ' European' have been seen intensely as mutually exclusive categories: so that idea of a European Muslim would be an impossibility. 'Muslim' and 'European' are not simply descriptive terms, their meaning cannot be reduced to dictionary definitions, rather they are to be understood as floating signifiers, around which there is a struggle to populate them with various signifieds. This metaphorical excess of 'Muslim' and 'European' points to the politicization of these labels since they operate as surface inscription for a wide range of demands and mobilizations that are not re-ducible to the facticity of being either European or Muslim. Islam and the West have become the names of antagonistic global projects, which increasingly polarize the world and

its history. It is in this context that the presence of populations in the European Union who increasingly define themselves and are defined by others as being Muslim assume a
critical importance. It is argued that the persistence of Muslims in Europe constitutes one of the gravest threats to European societies and cultures- it provides the sea via which
the jihadist infiltration of Europe can proceed. Thus, the
presence of Muslims qua Muslims has a general resonance
that resounds beyond the actuality of Muslims living in the
European Union. One way to resolve this dilemma has been
to articulate an European Islam. This approach comes from
various points of the political spectrum and includes both
those who are hostile to Islam and Muslims and those who
are not. So what could a European Islam look like?

One approach that we can immediately dismiss is one
that uses a geographical notion of Europe to locate European Islam be it in Andalusia, Islamicate Sicily or Bosnia or
including the 'indigenous' Muslim populations like Pomaks
in Bulgaria or Tartars in Finland. Historically, the idea of
what became Europe was based on the exclusion of any-
where under Islamicate control. It is important to understand that classification of landmasses in various continen-
tal permutations is not geological or geographical exercise.
The drawing of maps does not simply follow a dis-interest-
ed 'scientific' logic. Maps are not transparent and neutral
descriptions of what is already there, maps don't just report geographical boundaries, they formulate boundaries
reflecting cultural, historical and social imperatives. Thus
Europe (like Asia, or Africa or any other continent) is not
a geographical but rather a cartographic category, as such,
the boundaries of what we call Europe have not been constant or consistent. Our current identifications of some
territories as being European and others not, are the effect
of naturalization and cartographization of particular and
historical and cultural sensibilities, and not a transparent
reading of an objective reality. Islam in Andalusia or Sicily

or in the Balkan could only be considered to be European if we have an idea of the essence of European which is geographical and transhistorical.

Another approach we can reject fairly quickly understands European Islam as simply an empirical description. In other words, Muslims living in Europe are going to inflect their Islam with European accents. These inflections however do not constitute distinct "little Islams" (contra Al-Azmeh, Gilesanan).[1] At the most, we have rival projects to interpret a singular Islam. As I have emphasised in my writings it is precisely the existence of singular Islam as signifier that allows the constitution of Islamicate politics, in which Muslims (as well as non-Muslims) wage wars of interpretation to attach the signifier of Islam to the signified of their various specific projects. What remains to be devised is an account of Islam not reducible to these 'little Islams'. It is really not that interesting or that surprising to say that Islam in Egypt is different from Islam in Malaysia. What is to be explained, given all of the local interpretations of Islam is why it is that, when Egyptian Muslims practice Islam, they do so in the name of Islam - not an Egyptian variation. These "little Islams", when confronted by the global presence of Islam, are unable to account for this globality. We know Islam may be used as the means of articulating a multiplicity of positions. Dialectal variation is not sufficient to constitute a distinct language nor should it cause us to jump to the conclusion that these variations indicate distinct little Islams.

If we reject the cartographic and ethnographic description of European Islam as being either banal or flawed, then what, if anything, can be meant by the idea of a European Islam. To answer this question requires the abandonment of the primacy of the matrix of ontic studies. That is, studies that posit an essence that underpins (and

---

1   See Sayyid, 2003, for a critique of the notion of local little Islam, pp. 31-49.

predetermines) any subsequent investigation (Thomson, 2006). For the most part, depictions of Muslims in Europe (including official, journalistic, academic and popular) are represented in terms of an 'immigrant imaginary' (Sayyid, 2004; Hesse and Sayyid, 2006). In several articles and chapters, I have used the concept of 'immigrant imaginary' to account for the frequent way in which a small repertoire of tropes (conceptual, governmental, and cultural) are used to represent and regulate various ethnically marked settlers. This immigrant imaginary can at analytical level be considered to be defined by four key features.

The Immigrant Imaginary

First, the immigrant imaginary sees an ontological distinction between host society and the immigrants. This difference is marked in a variety of ways. The immigrants' food smells, their music is loud, their family structures are either anarchic or oppressive, their everyday conduct is different from "normal people." Whereas the host society has networks, immigrants have kinship, whereas the host society has modernity, the immigrants are tradition-bound. Or, for example, consider the way in which "settler" communities have too often been considered to be outside the pale of proper politics. It is thought that their activities can be explained in terms of "factionalism" or machinations of egotistical community leaders.

Secondly, the immigrant experiences are read from either an exoticised or banalizied register. The tendency to exoticize treats the immigrant as incarnating exceptionality: a manifestation of difference, expressed in signifiers of ritual, dress, and life in general. This is countered by the seemingly opposite tendency to make the immigrant the same. The bland sameness produced by banalization empties the Other of any particularity, by reducing the Other to a superstructual moment of a more general and deeper infrastructure. This may be defined in terms of either their genetic make-up, or their evolutionary development into the essence of what is human. In other words, under their (often darker) skins, immigrants are not different from the ethnically unmarked. There is nothing seriously distinctive about them. The exoticization of the immigrant works by treating every aspect of the immigrant experience as being distinct. The banalization of the immigrant works by considering the immigrant to be indistinct. Both these modes of appropriating the immigrant, despite their superficial opposition, are based on the assumption that the ethnically unmarked provide the norm by which the immigrant is to be judged. In other words, the ethnically unmarked represents the quintessential human.

Thirdly, the immigrant imaginary assumes that, with the passage of time, the ontological distinction between immigrant and host will be eroded as the host society consumes the immigrants. (This consumption is not purely metaphorical for the commercialisation of aspects of the immigrant experience, particularly in areas of cuisine and costume, are often cited as examples of how immigrants are being integrated into society, since their food and clothes are being sold to the general public). It assumes that, over time, immigrants will integrate into the host culture. The degree of integration into the host culture ranges from uncritical assimilation (in which the immigrant disappears without a trace into the host society) to equally un-theorized hybridization (in which the immigrant ends up being a hyphenated and hybridized member of the host community, i.e. adding colour and cuisine to the host society). Whatever route they take, these immigrants will find that all roads lead to their eventual elimination as distinct populations. Furthermore, the act of consumption by the host, will not substantively transform the host - the host remains the same. It is the immigrants who are chewed up and digested. This trope finds itself in speeches of politicians and commentaries of opinion-makers as exhortations to immigrants to speed up the process of assimilation by eliminating whatever practice is considered to be the current cause of moral panic e.g. arranged marriages, 'matriarchal' households, cultural schizophrenia or youth delinquency.

Fourthly, the form of this integration can be represented in discrete and successive stages called generations. A generation is one of the key units of analysis of this type of narrative. Generations are considered to be permanent units by which the immigration experience can be accounted for while continuing to maintain the status of immigrants. Generational differences are articulated as the crystallization of changes that immigrants are supposed to go through over time. Each generation marks the progress towards integration into the host community. The immigrant imaginary presents a picture analogous to the way in which tadpoles are transformed over time into full grown frogs. The use of the concept of generations within the immigrant imaginary performs two functions. First, it prevents the completion of the process of immigration. The prefixing of 'first', 'second' or 'third' to generation defers the moment when the immigrants can be considered settlers, i.e. fully part of the society in which they reside. The ethnically marked ex-colonial settlers become permanent immigrants. This act of freezing the immigrant to the moment at which he or she gets off the plane (or boat), has the effect of reinforcing the essentialization of the immigrant, since, regardless of how many generations have passed, the immigrant remains an immigrant, and the process of immigration remains without end. Thus, the moment of assimilation is continually deferred. The immigrants' relationship to the society in which they reside, remains that of newcomers. Second, the concept of generation works to de-historicize 'immigrants', to remove them from the currents of history, and thus excludes any political aspects of the 'immigrant' experience. Generations are deployed as a temporal category that removes any political dimension from any causal explanation. In other words, time is spatialized through the notion of generation. So the differences between the "first" and "second" generation are narrated as being due to the differences in assimilation into the host society and not as changes in historical context. The immigrant, over time, is to be transformed into a member of the host society (but, as was pointed out above, the transformation is never complete and constantly deferred).

The immigrant imaginary has a wide circulation both in academic and popular culture. It provides the tools by which the identity of 'immigrants' can be regulated and disciplined. It makes available the subject positions open to the immigrant communities and the conditions that underlie that opening. It is through the use of the idea of the immigrant imaginary that the usual stories about Muslims in European plutocracies are written and disseminated. Issues of cultural schizophrenia are read as forms of generational conflict, the notion of dual allegiances (e.g. currently the "problem" of being Muslim and Western), cruelty to animals, domestic violence and, of course, arranged marriages provide policy-makers, professional provocateurs and academics with a steady diet of shock horror stories and statements. The immigrant imaginary is essentialist, teleological, and ultimately xenophobic. While, ostensibly, it has prided itself in its ability to narrate the transformations arising out of the migration process, its ontology subverts its epistemological ambition. It is a paradigm of social change that is unable to account for change except as teleology. It is an attempt to understand social identities, which rests upon a pre-given "whatness" that is immutable and that determines the behaviour of both immigrants and hosts.

The immigrant imaginary provides the backdrop for the elaboration of a European Islam and European Muslims. This is because, the immigrant imaginary is deeply associated with postcolonial Europe. By postcolonial Europe,

I mean a Europe which has to deal with loss of its status as being the centre of a world order. The dis-mantling of the European colonial order, 'the loss of Empire' effected European societies, even those very few who did not have dominion over large populations described as non-European. The immigrant imaginary comes into play to order and comprehend the large scale immigration into Europe as its empires imploded. The immigrant imaginary is primarily deployed as means of policing postcolonial ethicised settlers.[2]

Ontically based analysis cannot provide a resolution of the Muslim question, since it leaves out any consideration about the process of subject formation of both Muslimness and Europeaness. A process which is at the forefront of current social developments. It is only by taking this ontological dimension into account that we can engage fully with very idea of European Islam. A European Islam that is not reducible to geographic or ethnographic descriptions requires an articulation between Europe and Islam at a conceptual level.

Euro-Islam?

There are two phases to this exercise, first an implicit list is made of values which are associated with Europe and Islam, and then these values are to be imported by Muslims into their guided engagement with Islam, to produce a European Islam. The difficulty, of course, arises from trying to come with characteristic values for the European or Islamicate enterprises which are little more than narcissistic fantasies dressed as essential truths. As nearly all projects to articulate European Islam assert the primacy of the European enterprise (hence calls to share values always demand transformation of Muslim practices but only a toleration

---

2   See the collection edited by N. Ali (et al.), *A Postcolonial People*, New York: Columbia University Press, 2006.

from European societies of Muslims) as such they depend on listing a cluster of values or cultural practices which are considered to be characteristic of European societies. These values are then used to exclude practices associated with Muslims. So in 2006, Charles Clarke, the then British Minister for the Interior, speaking in Washington, declared four core beliefs of Islamists that were totally antithetical to Western societies and which no Western government could ever accommodate. These included: defence of freedom of speech, gender equality, opposition to sharī`ah law and opposition to the establishment of the caliphate. The idea that European societies are characterised by freedom of speech or gender equality would be vulnerable to the criticism which demonstrates that freedom of speech is restricted not only through legislation (e.g. Holocaust denial) but also through 'sociological' factors such as oligopolistic control of media, etc. Similarly, gender equality is also undermined by various cultural factors. Nor would it be clear that distinction between Islamists and others could be organized in terms of opposition or acceptance of freedom of speech or gender equality. The attempt to intimidate Al-Jazeera or legislation introduced in the UK against the 'glorification of terrorism' all point to far more complicated positions in which the trope of 'freedom of speech' operates in the age of the 'war against terror'. As for gender equality the close relationship between the institutionalized gender apartheid of Saudi Arabia, has never been a significant hindrance to the description of the Saudi regime as moderate. Gender equality becomes a means of legitimating post-colonial 'humanitarian' interventions (Hirschkind Mahmood, 2002).[3] The Orientalism of this public intervention should be clear: Islam is being used as mirror of what is considered to be most valuable about Western cultural practices and historical trajectories.

---

3   Charles Hirschkind, Saba Mahmood, "Feminism, the Taliban, and Politics of Counter-Insurgency" *Anthropological Quarterly*, Vol. 75, No. 2 (Spring, 2002), pp. 339-354

The arguments for a European Islam, however, reject the relevance of Orientalism and instead focus on 'progressive, modern values' embedded in European (Union) social practices. Specifically, it is argued that Western practices such as freedom of speech, democratic constraints on the exercise of arbitrary power, and the de facto (if in many cases not de jure) separation between religious and state institutions will guarantee would allow Muslims to experiment in thought and deed about their creed, to reflect upon it an atmosphere free from opprobrium. This would create conditions for an Islamicate glasnost. European Islam, could act as a vanguard of reform for the rest of the Muslim Ummah.

This idea, however, is based on a rather generous understanding of Europe's 'democratic culture' and the attitude of European authorities in relation to Islam. The reason why the attitude of European governments towards Islamicate intellectual developments has been one of benign neglect was because they did not consider such developments to have any more significance than astrology conferences. In this, there was a clear difference to the government of Muslimistan for whom Islam remained of crucial importance, and they were, thus, unwilling to allow the free-flowing development of its interpretive literature. The argument in favour of a European Islam sees differences between Western and Non-Western attitudes to Islam in terms of difference in cultural values rather than in the area of political and security interests. No government in Muslimistan, even most resolutely 'secularist', could afford an attitude of benign neglect towards developments in Islamic thinking. This can be clearly seen in the Kemalist state's much vaunted separation of church and state only being accomplished by total state expansion to absorb all so-called religious institutions. Kemalist secularism is not a separation of mosque and state but rather a destruction of any independence of the mosque and its total internalisation within the bureaucratic structure of the state. It can also be clearly observed in the way in which, in the wake of the 'war on terror', Western plutocracies have increasingly sought to control and direct Muslim debates and interpretations of Islam. Secret police surveillance of Muslim intellectuals, regulation and censorship of Muslim freedom of expression, the use of torture (often outsourced), and extra-juridical measures are practices that are being used against Muslims in Europe as well in Muslimistan. The space of autonomous development of Islamicate interpretations has radically shrunk. European Islam cannot be the name of an interpretation of Islam that arises from the free play of Muslim debate and engagement.

For the articulation of a European Islam proceeds from a denial of the universality of Islam, while promoting subordination to Europeaness. European Islam becomes another instance of Orientalism in which Islam acts as a counter-factual mirror to narcissistic fantasies of an exceptional European grandness. Two major points can be made specifically in relation to the project of European Islam.

Firstly, the project begins by accepting (either implicitly or explicitly) that Islam is a religion whereas religions are basically what Western Christianity became following wars of reformation and counter-reformation. Islam, because it does not fit into this idea of religion, is considered deviant or even immature and thus needs to be refashioned in order to accord with this European Enlightenment based definition. Euro-Islam is the name of a version of Islam which would be acceptable to this European Enlightenment conceptualization of religion.

Secondly, this European Enlightenment concept of religion is based on a series of assumptions which sees European history as universal history. In other words, developments in European cultural practices are assumed to have relevance for all other cultural formations. As I have written elsewhere this is clearly seen in the way in arguments which are often presented in favour of secularism. [4] Secularism's supposed benefits can be grouped under three broad headings:

1. Epistemological arguments based around the claim that without secularism there can be no scientific progress, and without scientific progress there could be no technological advances. In this sense, secularism as an epistemological category rather than a social one can be described as denoting a shift from an episteme centred on God to one centred on man (sic). The core of the argument is that secularism de-legitimates the claims of religious authorities to control the production of knowledge, and creates the conditions for the rejection of ontological claims found in sacred narratives in favour of a scientifically approved ontology (Sayyid, 2008)

2. Secularism is necessary to ensure civic peace and social harmony and to prevent religious passions from getting out of hand. By separating religion and confining it to the private sphere, secularism prevents differences in religious opinions from becoming a source of conflict that would engulf a society's public space. Religious differences become matters of individual taste and therefore have little impact upon the organisation of social life at large. In addition, secularism prevents contending groups from making appeals to supernatural forces as a way of reinforcing their positions and keeps all parties on an open playing field in which debate cannot be short-circuited by such appeals (ibid).

3. Secularism presents the necessary pre-condition for the exercise of democracy – which following Lefort's useful understanding is based on keeping the space of power empty (1986:279). The 'removal' of God allows the space of power to be emptied. The claim is that democracy is government that is ultimately based on the idea of the 'sovereignty of the people' (regardless of how this idea is expressed in reality e.g.

---

4   The following section is taken from Sayyid (2008).

in Britain it is parliament which is sovereign not the people, however, the power of parliament derives from the people...). Popular sovereignty seems to preclude any place for the idea of a sovereign God or a sovereign priesthood. Thus the benefits of secularism help to define modernity itself. Modernity, of course, remains a narrative about Western exceptionality (Sayyid, 2003: 101-102), thus secularism becomes a marker of Western identity. The epistemological, civic and democratic arguments for secularism are formulated as part of a narrative of Western exceptionally (ibid).

European Islam is an Islam that can be accommodated within the Western notions of secularism and its presumed benefits. Specifically, the applicability of the three main arguments for secularism and their relevance for Muslims can be challenged by focusing on experience of autonomous Islamicate cultural formations- that is those cultural formations that existed prior to the colonial enframing of the planet. In other words, the shift from Western to Islamicate societies seemingly undermines the universal claims for secularism.

So, for example, the idea of the epistemological case for secularism rests upon a conflict between science and church – a conflict symbolized by the trials of Galileo. The absence of an organized church made drawing such clear demarcations between the authority of religion and science difficult within Islamicate societies. Perhaps, more importantly, the epistemological case for the benefits of secularism on the assumption that the understanding of the Divine in Islamic and Christian discourses is homologous. In the Christianological concept of the Divine, the Human and Divine occupy the same plane, thus human endeavour can potentially compete with the Divine. The conjoining of human and divine spheres as described through the category of incarnation in which divine and mundane fuse in body of Christ no doubt helps to sustain a perspective in which human and divine exist at the same plane. Thus narratives of Divine causality and intervention are locked in zero-sum game with narratives that centre on human agency. As a consequence, science and religion continually collide within Christianological narratives. Within Islamic interpretations the Divine and human cannot be bridged. Islamicate reflections on the nature of the Divine have been very consistent in maintaining the gap between human and Divine spheres, a gap that is wide and permanent. While this in contrast between Christianological and Islamicate discourse on the Divine cannot be seen as essential or foundational- since, differences in reflection on the Divine indicate contingent conversations within various hermeneutic traditions, and not the uncovering of specific essences which are 'hard-wired' within Christianity or Islam. (After all, many early Christian sectarian disputes often had a Christological element e.g. controversies between those who accepted the interpretations of the Council of Chalcedon, and those such as the Arians, Nestorians and Monophysites) (ibid).

The case for secularism as necessary for civic peace is largely based on extrapolating from the European experiences of the wars of the reformation and counter-reformation to make general points about the relationship between civic peace and de-politicization of religious belief. As has been pointed out, there is no direct analogue to sectarian warfare of such intensity and scale in Islamicate history and thus the idea that civic peace is only possible if religion is confined to the private sphere cannot be simply read from Islamicate history.[5] It is possible to make the very opposite case, the retreat of religion from the public sphere in Islamicate history has been most often associated with the breakdown of civic peace. For example, the oft admired secularist order in Turkey was imposed from the top, upon an exhausted war weary population- secularism of the Turkish republic was not a

---

5   The closest approximation is the conflict between the Fatimids and Abbasids, however, the infrastructural capacity of both Abbasid and Fatimid political orders were not sufficient to produce such an intensive form of violence- as experienced in the wars of religion in Europe.

response to demands of the Turkish masses but rather the desires of the Kemalist elite's authorities' project of Westernization. Secularism in the context of Islamicate communities has often meant de-Islamization and, for the most part, has been imposed either by colonial regimes or Westernizing regimes- these projects have all served to increase rather than reduce social conflict. Empirically, the scale and intensity of violence in Muslim countries which have been ruled avowedly as secular regimes has been such that it would not inspire much confidence about any association between secularism and civic peace. (ibid)

The argument that secularism is a necessary pre-condition of any political system of popular sovereignty ignores the possible ways in which popular sovereignty can be finessed from the example of various constitutional monarchies to the suggestion by Mawdudi and others who re-described popular will as being viceregal rather than sovereign. In other words, the sovereignty of the Divine is the elaboration of the centrality of God to the cosmos but cannot be practical sovereignty in the formulation suggested by Carl Schmitt ('the sovereign is who decides upon the exception') if for no other reason than the idea of a monotheistic version of the omnipotent and omniscient God does not allow for the Divine to have any exception.

It would seem that the meaning of secularism is perhaps to be found in attachment to a Plato-to-NATO sequence that encapsulates Western-ness. Thus, the articulation of a global Muslim subjectivity contributes to the provincialization of Europe's final vocabulary, by threatening to reveal Plato-to-NATO as histographical convention rather than history. In context of Muslims living in Western plutocracies the staples of the 'immigrant imaginary' becomes strained, as categories such as religion, minority, 'race' etc. are increasingly seen as part of the Plato-to-NATO sequence.

The validity of this sequence rests upon the exercise of coloniality. European Islam is based on maintaining and reinforcing the distinction between West and Non-West which is constitutive of the colonial enframing of the world. It seeks to regulate and discipline Muslim demands for autonomy by reference to Europeaness.

The articulation of a global Muslim subjectivity challenges the universality of the Western enterprise by questioning its assumption that the history of the West is the destiny of the world. This is precisely the assumption that underlies Tibi's work. It is in this light, Tibi's intervention can be read as belonging to the genre of Western supremacist discourse which assumes that European history is universal history. In other words, developments in European cultural practices are assumed to have relevance for all other cultural formations. Of course, in the age of the 'war on terror', this means that European cultural practices are the antidote to the articulation of Muslim autonomy. Tibi's Euro-Islam, asserts the primacy of the European enterprise, a disposition which is reflected in his call that in order to share values Muslims must transform their practices and learn what is absent from their culture: pluralism, while European societies already have pluralism and just need to apply it more consistently (ibid:140).

A trawl through the cells of Guantanamo and other secret prisons of the America's global gulag would demonstrate that cultural and ethnic pluralism is not absent in the ranks of Islamists and certainly is not absent among Islamicate societies.[6] Rather, it is the discourse of Western-inspired nationalism with its insistence on one government, one people and one land which has in very recent history sought to erase pluralism, often with genocidal ferocity.

---

6   The term Islamicate was coined by Marshall Hodgson to refer "...to social and cultural complex historically associated with Islam and the Muslims, both among Muslims themselves and even when found among non-Muslims."Hodgson, 1978:59. Hodgson distinguishes Islamicate from Islamic which he see directly derived from Islam's sacral texts, rather being simply inspired by them (ibid:57-60).

Tibi believes that a "Euro-Islam" is necessary to further integration and social cohesion. Euro-Islam will enable Muslims in Europe to become European Muslims. That is, being Muslim will become another life-style adding to the superficial diversity of other life-styles available in Western plutocracies. The Muslim subject position is simply colonized by European expectations and demands of what a good Muslim should be. This good European Muslim, it is argued, is not only necessary to preserve social cohesion in Europe's urban centres but a good European Muslim is also the true essence of what a good Muslims should be (ibid: 144,146-147). The idea of Euro-Muslim as distinct from other Muslims is based on the assumptions of Western supremacist discourse. It fails to acknowledge the possibility that universal values and notions of good life can be generated from any historical community, that they do not require the imitation of the European experience. In other words, westernization is not a necessary precursor to improvements in social well-being. Ultimately, Euro-Islam is based on maintaining and reinforcing the distinction between the West and the Non-West which is constitutive of the colonial en-framing of the world. It seeks to regulate and discipline Muslim demands for autonomy by reference to Europeaness.

Conclusion

If Islam is not a religion as the European Enlightenment's dominant discourse would demand then how are we to understand it. Perhaps one way would be to see Islam as inaugurating a distinct historical community. Islam began with a series of revelations received by the Prophet Muhammad (570-632) during the 610s (CE). The nature of these revelations has a family resemblance to many tropes found within the cultural milieu of the Nile to Oxus region, which can also be found at work in Jewish and Christian sacred stories. Islam orders these narratives of Abrahamic monotheism, placing itself as the culmination of a series of revelations associated with a diverse group of Prophets such as Abraham, Moses and Jesus. Islam inaugurated a new semantic universe, which succeeded, initially, radically transforming large parts of the Afro-Eurasian landmass so that these themes that continued beyond the arrival of Islam could only do so through a cultural lexicon dominated by the venture of Islam. Islam is language as well as a historical sequence by which Muslims can project themselves into the past and the future. It is like other major historical communities able to generate the universal from the cultivation of its "own" language games.

Thus the emergence of substantial Muslim minorities within the boundaries of the European Union plutocracies has raised a number of doubts regarding the confident expectation that Islam would wither away as the global advance of westernisation brought secularisation and modernization in its wake. Not only has Islam failed to follow the trajectory pursued by variants of Christianity, namely depoliticisation and confinement to the private sphere, but it has, in contrast, forcefully re-asserted its public presence in the world. The continued and growing significance of Islam has three aspects to it. Firstly, there is the geopolitical dimension defining and organizing a series of mobilizations against the contemporary world order. Secondly, there is an epistemological aspect since the persisting relevance of Islam suggests that the history of the world cannot simply be presented as a scaled up version of the history of the West. This combination of geopolitical and epistemological challenge is partly responsible for creating the third aspect: that of cultural challenge in which the contemporary assertion of Islam raises questions about European identity and destiny. In light of these developments, the recycling of conventional narratives about Islam seems redundant and increasingly problematic.

It is not clear what an articulation of a European Islam would achieve apart from maintaining and reinforcing the frontier between Europeaness and Non-Europeaness, since, for a European Islam to be viable, it would have to be distinguished from a Non-European Islam. As has been pointed out, the 'violent hierarchy' between Europeaness and Non-Europeaness is constitutive of Western racism. The idea of European Islam belongs to an age in which the ability of Muslims to write their history was constrained by Westphalian order in which nation-states were able to regulate flows of peoples and information. An European Islam is difficult to sustain in the context of a planet unified by neo-liberal economic integration, and neo-conservative military expansion. Any attempt to fit the various mobilizations in the name of Islam into a European shaped hole, does not recognize the postcolonial temper of the times. The movements and struggles for Muslim autonomy have become globalized. In the struggle for Muslim autonomy, the various attempts to produce domesticated interpretations of Islam are unlikely to be successful. The attempt to domesticate Islam is considered to be legitimate because of dangers that are assumed to arise from it. At the heart of this danger is the possibility that Muslims may write their own history and thus displace the claims that world history is simply an upscaled version of Western history. The fate of European Islam is unlikely to be any different than the fate of a Saudi Islam or an Anatolian Islam; Islam has escaped in the general field of Muslim discursively. Only liberation of Muslimness and the establishment of overarching political structures are going to be successful in regulating the war of interpretations being waged around Islam. Such structures are only likely to be established in the name of Islam itself.

REFERENCES

El-Ariss, Tarek, (2007) The Making of an Expert: The Case of Irshad Manji. The Muslim World, vol. 97, January, pp. 93-110.

Finney, N., and L Simpson., *Sleepwalking to Segregation?: Challenging Myths About Race and Migration*, Bristol: Policy Press, 2009.

Hesse, B., 2007. 'Racialized Modernity: An analytics of white mythologies', *Ethnic and Racial Studies*, Volume 30, No. 4 pp. 643-663

Hirschkind, Charles, and Saba Mahmood, "Feminism, the Taliban, and Politics of Counter-Insurgency" *Anthropological Quarterly*, Vol. 75, No. 2 (Spring, 2002), pp. 339-354.

Hodgson, M., *The Venture of Islam*, vol. 1, Chicago: University of Chicago Press, 1977.

Sabet, Amr G.E, *Islam and the Political: Theory, Governance and International Relations*, London: Pluto Press, 2008.

Sayyid, S. *A Fundamental Fear: Eurocentrism and the Emergence of Islamism*, London: Zed Books, 1997 [2003].

Sayyid, S. "Bad Faith: Anti-Essentialism and Universalism" in Avtar Brah and Annie. E. Coombes (eds.), *Hybridity and it Discontents*, London: Routledge, 2000.

Sayyid, S. "Slippery People: The Immigrant Imaginary and the Grammar of Colour." in Ian Law, Deborah Phillips and Laura Turney (eds.) *Institutional Racism in Higher Education*, London: Trentham Books Ltd, 2004.

Sayyid, S. "The Secular, the Political, and the Limits of the Multicultural', in Levey and Modood (eds) *Secularism, Religion and Multicultural Citizenship*, Cambridge University Press, 2008.

Sayyid, S. "Answering the Muslim Question" CERS Working Paper. University of Leeds, 2009.

Sayyid, S. *Recalling the Caliphate*, London: Hurst, 2014.

Tibi, Bassam, 2010. "Ethnicity of Fear? Islamic Migration and the Ethnicization of Islam in Europe", *Studies in Ethnicity and Nationalism*, Vol. 10, No. 1 pp. 126-157.

Kommentar

Dr. Jörn Thielmann (Deutschland)

Meine sehr verehrten Damen und Herren,[1]

ich bin gebeten worden, auf Deutsch zu kommentieren und ich danke für die Einladung. Ich finde, es ist eine große Herausforderung, der Sie sich da stellen. (I'm also very grateful, Mr. Sayyid, for your paper, which was for me quite thought-provoking and stimulating for controversial debate.) Ich stimme Dr. Sayyid aus verschiedenen Gründen in vielen Punkten nicht zu und ich werde versuchen, in einem Durchgang durch seinen Vortrag die wichtigsten Punkte für mich anzusprechen, und auch versuchen, mich auf die konkrete Situation von Muslimen in Deutschland zu beziehen. Es ist klar, wenn wir über Europäer und Muslime sprechen, bewegen wir uns in einem politisch hochaufgeladenen Bereich. Das sind keine neutralen Begriffe mehr, sondern Begriffe, die mittlerweile eine sehr emotionale und sehr aggressiv aufgeladene Konnotation haben, wo heftige Kämpfe auf den unterschiedlichsten Gebieten in den Medien, auf der politischen Ebene, aber auch durchaus auf lokaler Ebene toben. Wir sind hier in Bonn, Köln ist nicht weit, den deutschen Teilnehmern muss der Konflikt um den großen, geplanten Moscheebau in Köln-Ehrenfeld nicht in Erinnerung gerufen werden.

Am Schluss hat Dr. Sayyid davon gesprochen, dass Islam (ein) Islam ist, oder der Islam eine Größe an sich ist.

---

[1] Ich danke Arne Greifsmühlen für die Erstellung einer druckfähigen Version des Vortragmitschnittes.

Das stimmt natürlich, aber Islam – das ist jetzt vielleicht meine ethnologische Sicht, oder soziologische Sicht – Islam wird gelebt von Muslimen. Das klingt zunächst banal, aber das bedeutet, dass man durchaus in Blick nehmen muss, dass Muslime in konkreten und verschiedenen Lebenswelten leben und dass die Verhältnisse von Muslimen auch hier in Europa sehr verschiedene sind. Das ist ein Unterschied, ob Sie als Muslime in England, in Frankreich, in Luxemburg oder hier in Deutschland leben. Und ich würde die Idee aufgreifen, die heute Morgen Parvez Manzoor aufgebracht hat, um zu sagen, am besten ist es, wenn wir von Muslimen ausgehen. Das wäre dann für eine wissenschaftliche Untersuchung bedeutungsvoll (und da widerspreche ich Dr. Sayyid, denn ich halte ethnographische Studien für sehr sinnvoll und die können natürlich nur lokal sein). In einem ersten Schritt sollte man fragen: Wie ist die Lebenswelt von Muslimen, wie ist die Vorstellungswelt von Muslimen, was treibt sie um, was ist ihnen wichtig, wie sind ihre Erfahrungen? Das ist wichtig, um nicht rückwärts in die Falle einer Essentialisierung zu fallen. Und Dr. Sayyid scheint in seinem Paper in vielen Punkten in die ontologische essentialisierende Falle getappt zu sein. Ich kann von meinem eigenen Fach Islamwissenschaften nur sagen: Diejenigen, die sozialwissenschaftlich arbeiten, haben die Kritik des Orientalismus von Edward Said gründlich gelernt und verinnerlicht, und bemühen sich durchaus, orientalistische Diskurse über Muslime und über „den Islam" zu vermeiden.

Was mir auch zu kurz gekommen zu sein scheint, ist die simple Realität, dass Muslime in Europa, Muslime in Deutschland, in sehr spezifischen Kontexten sozialisiert werden. Sie werden in bestimmten Familien geboren oder werden in bestimmten Familien groß. Es gibt sozio-ökonomische Bedingungen, es gibt – das ist jetzt natürlich eine sehr ethnologische Perspektive – Einflüsse darauf, zum Beispiel durch die Schulbildung, wie Muslime auch selbst ihren Glauben und ihr Leben konzeptualisieren können.

Wie sie – möglicherweise in einer Spaltung zwischen „traditioneller muslimischer Theologie" oder muslimischen Traditionen – Islam konzeptualisieren, und muslimisches Leben konzeptualisieren und darüber sprechen. Aber auch in der deutschen, französischen etc. Denkkultur und Denkweise, die ja wirkmächtig ist. Das ist natürlich auch in Bezug auf Schulen der Fall. Schulen sind Anstalten der Disziplinierung; nicht nur körperlich, sondern auch geistig. Das hat Auswirkung auf die Diskurse von Muslimen, die durch diese europäische, diese deutsche (oder was auch immer) Schule gegangen sind. Das war der erste Punkt.

Der zweite Punkt ist: Muslime sind konfrontiert mit öffentlichen Praktiken und Diskursen und können sich davon nicht freimachen. Es gibt in Deutschland immer diese große Debatte über Parallelgesellschaften, die Idee, dass da jetzt irgendwelche isolierten Gemeinschaften existieren würden, die völlig abgeschottet sind und die überhaupt keinen Kontakt mit anderen haben. Aber das ist eine Illusion, das ist eine politische Dämonisierung von muslimischen Lebensverhältnissen. Es entspricht nicht der Realität. Muslime müssen sich positionieren und sind beeinflusst von diesen Diskursen. Ich denke, ich muss im Rahmen einer Veranstaltung von Millî Görüş nicht groß ausführen, was das bedeutet. Denn Sie sind pausenlos, wenn Sie mit der Öffentlichkeit kommunizieren, mit diesen Diskursen konfrontiert. Und Sie erfahren das auch sehr lebensweltlich; wir haben vor kurzem Ramadan gehabt: Fasten in einer Gesellschaft, wo Muslime nicht die Mehrheit sind, wo die entsprechenden kulturell-religiösen Traditionen nicht präsent sind, ist ein starker Willensakt. Das ist meines Erachtens ein stärkerer Willensakt, als wenn Sie in Ägypten oder in Jordanien, oder in bestimmten Teilen in der Türkei leben und fasten.

Und was, denke ich, auch berücksichtigt werden muss, ist die Erfahrung – das klang schon in dem Vortrag von Stephano Allievi an – muslimischer Vielfalt. Die betrifft vielleicht eher homogene türkische Gruppierungen wie Millî Görüş, weniger aber alle anderen Muslime, die in Deutschland oder Europa leben, die zahlenmäßig nicht so stark vertreten sind, dass sie jetzt irgendwie ihr eigenes Süppchen kochen können, in Form von Vereinen oder Moscheen. Muslime erfahren Vielfalt. Sie begegnen auf einmal hier unterschiedlichen Praktiken. Das bedeutet nicht, dass es nicht – und das ist ein wichtiger Punkt, den Dr. Sayyid gemacht hat – ein universales Referenzsystem „Islam" gäbe. Aber das bedeutet trotz alledem, dass man im Alltag und in der Lebens- und Glaubenspraxis durchaus aushandeln muss, wie denn beispielsweise die gemeinsame Praxis einer Moschee sein soll. Man muss sich dann entsprechend positionieren. Und es scheint interessant zu sein, und ich werde da gleich noch mal näher darauf eingehen.

Ich bin absolut einverstanden mit Dr. Sayyid, Euroislam, European Islam - und da bin ich nicht einverstanden mit Stephano Allievi – als Kategorien erstmal über Bord zu werfen. Es gibt den gelebten Islam von Muslimen in Europa, ja, aber alles andere, diese normative Konstruktion à la Bassam Tibi eines Euroislam halte ich, wenn ich das ganz grob sagen soll, einfach für Schwachsinn. Bassam Tibi wehrt sich dann dagegen, dass das, was er da als Euroislam propagiert, als eine Ein-Mann-Religion bezeichnet wird, aber es kommt dem ziemlich nahe.

Sehr wichtig finde ich die Bemerkung von Dr. Sayyid über dieses Imaginäre der Migrationserfahrung. Besonders fruchtbar finde ich seine Beobachtung der Etikettierung von Generationen. Es scheint so zu sein, dass diese Etikettierung nur bei Muslimen vorgenommen wird, nicht bei anderen Migrantenkommunitäten, oder bei anderen Migrantenkommunitäten nicht in gleicher Weise. Bestimmte Probleme, die Muslime in dieser Gesellschaft haben, also soziale Probleme, Jugendkriminalität, häusliche Gewalt etc., auch manchmal schlechte berufliche Integrationschancen, zum Teil niedriger Ausbildungsstand etc., finden sich bei anderen Migrantenkommunitäten genauso. Im deutschen Kontext hat vor kurzem Mark Terkessidis darauf hingewiesen und es illustriert mit Beispielen aus der italienischen, griechischen etc. Kommunität. Wir sprechen auch nicht mehr beispielsweise von der dritten oder vierten Generation der Polen im Ruhrgebiet. Ich bin im Ruhrgebiet groß geworden und als Kind war „Polacke" noch ein Schimpfwort, und das spielt heute keine Rolle mehr. Ich befürchte fast, wir werden leider diese positive Entwicklung, dass Diskriminierungsbegriffe aus dem aktiven Wortschatz verschwinden, in Bezug auf Muslime wahrscheinlich noch längere Zeit nicht erleben dürfen. Also ich denke, es ist ein wichtiger Hinweis zu sagen, dass dieses Generationsmodell nicht mehr greift. Ich beobachte in Feldforschungen durchaus auch starke, geistige Entwicklungen der ersten Generation türkischer Migranten. Insofern klingt da bei mir sofort etwas an.

Was allerdings ein Problem ist, da hat Stephano Allievi auch schon darauf hingewiesen, ist die Ethnisierung des Islam. Ein ganz fundamentales, praktisches Problem scheint zu sein – zumindest in Deutschland, ich kenne diese Situation in anderen Ländern nur ansatzweise aus der Forschungsliteratur, aber nicht aus eigenen Erleben –: Man ist nicht mehr Türke, also man ist nicht mehr türkischer Herkunft oder pakistanischer Herkunft oder gegebenenfalls auch schwarzafrikanischer Herkunft, man ist Muslim. Man wird als solcher etikettiert und man ist verantwortlich für „den" Islam und „die Muslime" – egal, ob man selbst religiös ist oder nicht, das spielt überhaupt keine Rolle. Sie können Atheist sein und als Muslim wahrgenommen werden und müssen sich für den Islam und die Muslime an und für sich auf dieser ganzen weiten Erde erklären. Das sind Prozesse, die gerade auch für die Identitätsbildung junger Menschen hochproblematisch sind. Ich nenne das in Anklang an das berühmte Theaterstück von Marx Frisch das Andorraphänomen, also dieses „Labelling". Sie werden konstant gezwungen, ob Sie wollen oder nicht, sich in Bezug auf den

Islam und islamische Religiosität zu positionieren und das hat Folgen. Und das greift natürlich den Punkt, den Dr. Sayyid auch machte, über die Prozesse der Subjektformierung sowohl eines Muslimseins und eines Europäerseins, auf.

Bezüglich der Rückwirkung europäischer muslimischer Diskurse auf die islamische Welt: Ich beobachte eine zunehmende Vernetzung. Es wurde schon kurz der European Council for Fatwa and Research von Scheich Yusuf al-Qaradawi und dieser ganze Versuch, wo auch Tariq Ramadan und andere involviert sind, einen *Fiqh al-Aqalliyat* zu entwickeln, einen „Fiqh der Minderheiten", angesprochen. Angesichts der Tatsache, dass die Welt, ob man will oder nicht, sich global zunehmend vernetzt und gerade für junge Muslime das Internet eine enorme Ressource darstellt, kann ich mir nicht vorstellen, dass Fatawas, also Rechtsgutachten, die Yusuf al-Qaradawi für eine spezifisch europäische Situation formuliert, nicht von arabischen, türkischen, malaiischen oder sonst welchen Muslimen zur Kenntnis genommen werden, und dass sie dann nicht wahrnehmen, dass er durchaus für ähnliche Sachverhalte in unterschiedlichen geographischen Settings unterschiedliche Antworten gibt. Ich beobachte auch durchaus die Orientierung, auch von Muslimen in Deutschland, an solchen globalen Diskursen weltweit. Wir können Phänomene beobachten unter jungen Muslimen in Ägypten genauso wie in Deutschland, da gibt es keine größeren Unterschiede, scheint mir.

Zum Komplex Säkularisierung: Es war mir zu oft zu schnell von „The West" die Rede, von dem Westen. Europa scheint mir – und das kam am Ende von Dr. Sayyids Vortrag und Paper ja auch zum Ausdruck – ein sehr deutlicher Sonderfall zu sein. In Amerika scheint die Situation meines Erachtens eine andere zu sein. Vor kurzem war ich auf einer Podiumsdiskussion mit amerikanischen Wissenschaftlern und auch amerikanischen Muslimen über Säkularismus/Säkularisierung in Europa und Amerika. Religion spielt eine ganz andere Rolle in den USA, alleine schon deshalb, weil

Amerika sich geformt hat durch europäische religiöse Minderheiten. Da konnte keiner dem anderen vorschreiben, wo
es langgeht. Und es scheint mir, dass Dr. Sayyid in seiner
Auflistung dieser Säkularisierungsideen, also was Säkularisierung und Säkularismus an sich leistet, übersehen hat,
dass Säkularisierung, Säkularismus im europäischen Kontext auch Gleichheit der Religion zur Folge hatte, was auch
eine Chance für den Islam ist, wenn man es ernst nimmt.

Mit Stephano Allievi würde ich dann auch noch mal
unangenehme Fragen stellen. Wie sieht es denn aus mit der
Behandlung von Apostaten, sozusagen geborenen Muslimen, die sagen, ich habe mit Religion, mit dem Islam nichts
mehr am Hut, ich wechsle zu einer anderen Religion oder
zu überhaupt keiner Religion? Wie geht die innermuslimi-
sche Debatte damit um? Das ist durchaus ein Problem. Auf
muslimischer Seite solchen Fragen offensiv zu begegnen,
wäre eine Möglichkeit, Opferrollenmuster zu überwinden.
Für Europa, denke ich, ist es tatsächlich so, dass es eine
enge Verbindung von staatlicher Organisation und Religion
gibt. Vor kurzem hat Armando Salvatore seine Habilitati-
onsschrift auf Englisch dazu vorgelegt. Die Europäer, denke
ich, halten sich für säkularer als sie sind. Es ist natürlich so,
dass die westliche Moderne, oder die Moderne, ein spezifisch westliches Projekt ist und dass Macht sehr ungleich
verteilt ist. Macht liegt eindeutig – ökonomische Macht,
militärische Macht, und deswegen auch durchaus intellek-
tuelle Definitionsmacht – auf Seiten der USA und Europas,
und das stellt natürlich ein Problem dar.

Vielleicht abschließend nur noch die Frage, was die
angemahnte muslimische Autonomie denn konkret be-
deuten kann? Also wie sollen wir uns muslimische Autonomie im Kontext europäischer Gesellschaften, im Kontext
allgemeiner politischer Aushandlungsprozesse in europäischen Gesellschaften, beispielsweise in Deutschland, vorstellen? Welche Modelle sollen wir aufgreifen? Für mich
ist es überhaupt keine Frage, dass der Islam und Muslime

in Europa dauerhaft präsent sind, dass ihnen ein Platz zukommt und zwar ein würdiger Platz, ohne dass sie darum betteln müssen. Aber das bedeutet gleichermaßen auch, dass Muslime sich, und da greife ich Dr. Canatan auf, natürlich auch Gedanken darüber machen müssen, was denn die Furcht und die Sorgen auf europäischer Seite sind, und versuchen müssen, auch diese Furcht zu verstehen, um ihre eigene Position auch besser im öffentlichen Raum vertreten zu können.

Vielen Dank für Ihre Aufmerksamkeit. Ich bin gespannt auf die Diskussion.

Muslime in Europa

Oğuz Üçüncü (Deutschland)

Die Islamische Gemeinschaft Millî Görüş steht als Religionsgemeinschaft mit einer nunmehr, zählt man die „Vorläufer-Organisationen" hinzu, fast 40-jährigen Geschichte im Spannungsfeld der heute und hier diskutierten Themengebiete. Dabei ist die Verbandsgeschichte natürlich eng verwoben mit der Migrationsgeschichte türkischer Arbeitskräfte, die zunächst für einen begrenzten Zeitraum aus ökonomischen Gründen nach Europa kamen. Es war nicht die „Bildungselite" der Türkei, die ihr Glück in Europa versuchen wollte, nein, es waren vor allem Angehörige sogenannter „bildungsferner Schichten", die dem Ruf europäischer Arbeitgeber gefolgt sind. Dass bei ihrer Auswahl ihre körperliche Statur mehr als ihr geistiges Potential als Kriterium diente, ist ein Fakt, den die erste Einwanderergeneration mit einem bittersüßen Lächeln bestätigt.

Die diversen Entwicklungsstufen, -also zunächst befristete Bleibeabsicht, Familiennachzug und dann dauerhafte Bleibeabsicht-, die dem Anwerbeabkommen mit der Türkei folgten, sind bekannt und wurden an verschiedener Stelle wissenschaftlich beschrieben. Ein Aspekt, der bei der Aufarbeitung der Migrationsgeschichte aus unserer Sicht nicht ausreichend gewürdigt wird, aber für die Entwicklung eines islamischen Gemeindelebens in Europa maßgeblich war, ist, dass der türkische Staat die nach Europa ausgewanderten Menschen bis in die 80er Jahre hinein in ihren religiösen Belangen sich selbst überlassen hat. Was auf den ersten Blick im europäischen

Kontext selbstverständlich erscheint, dass nämlich Religion von Religionsgemeinschaften organisiert wird, ist es, mit Blick auf die institutionelle Verwurzelung des Islams in den Staatsstrukturen der Türkei, dann doch nicht mehr.

So spielte in unserer eigenen Verbandsgeschichte bei der Gründung der ersten Moscheevereine und Dachverbände die religiöse Grundversorgung der muslimischen Zuwanderer zwar eine wichtige Rolle, dennoch galt von Anfang an hinsichtlich der inhaltlichen Ausgestaltung der Anspruch, „die alten Zöpfe" im Sinne eines als tradiert und staatlich reglementiert empfundenen Religionsverständnisses abzuschneiden. Stattdessen sollte immer mehr der türkische Begriff „şuur", also das bewusste Praktizieren des Glaubens, in den Mittelpunkt der Glaubens- und Lebenspraxis treten.

Vieles wurde hinterfragt, wobei die zentralen Fragen lauteten: Was erwartet der Schöpfer von mir? Welche Verantwortung resultiert daraus für mich und für meine Rolle in der Gesellschaft? Wie werde ich dieser Verantwortung gerecht?

Im Lichte dieser Fragen galt der für die türkische Gesellschaft typische unbedingte Obrigkeitsgehorsam und die Verbannung des Religiösen in die Privatsphäre als nicht länger hinnehmbar. „Der Islam war mehr als nur Privatsache" zwischen Schöpfer und Geschöpf, er hatte eine gesellschaftliche Dimension und der galt es Gehör zu verschaffen. Das sagte man nicht nur in Deutschland und Europa, sondern natürlich auch in der Türkei. Um Missverständnisse schon im Vorfeld auszuräumen, an diesen Positionen hat sich bis heute nichts geändert und wird sich auch in Zukunft nichts ändern.

Dennoch ist der beschriebene grundsätzliche Gestus wichtig, um unser Selbstverständnis in der Gründungsphase unseres Verbandes nachzuvollziehen. In einer Zeit, in der es scheinbar nur die Wahl zwischen dem kapitalistischen Westen und dem kommunistischen Osten gab, schickte sich eine neue Generation von Muslimen an, eine Alternative zu diesen Systemen aufzuzeigen. Weder der Westen noch der Osten allein konnte nach diesem Verständnis die Antworten auf die brennenden Fragen dieser Zeit liefern. Es waren die eigenen religiösen Quellen, denen man sich „bewusster" zuwenden musste und schon offenbarte sich eine unerschöpfliche Bandbreite von Lösungsmöglichkeiten für die Probleme der Welt.

Mit dem Untergang der Sowjetunion und der Kapitulation des Kommunismus als ideologische Alternative vergrößerte sich die Gewissheit für den eigenen Ansatz. Der Islam war nun die einzige Alternative zu all den Konzepten und Werten, die uns der über den Kommunismus obsiegende Westen zu bieten hatte.

Dabei speiste sich die Ablehnung dieser Werte nicht vornehmlich aus einer religiös fundierten Auseinandersetzung mit den selbigen, sondern vor allem aus der in der politischen Praxis an den Tag gelegten Doppelmoral in puncto Demokratie, Marktwirtschaft und Menschenrechte. Dieser Doppelmoral entzog der Islam mit dem ihm ureigenen Grundprinzip der „Gerechtigkeit" den Boden. Dementsprechend galt es als gewiss, dass Muslime im Lichte eines „gerechten" Ansatzes dauerhaft wahre Demokratie, wahre Marktwirtschaft und wahre Menschenrechte als Quell von Frieden und Wohlstand für die Menschheit gewährleisten können.

Bei einer nüchternen Betrachtung im Jahre 2007 kann man konstatieren, dass es nach wie vor eine tiefe, auch religiös begründete Überzeugung gibt, dass auf der Grundlage eines richtig praktizierten Islams Frieden und Gerechtigkeit hergestellt werden können. Das „Wie" ist jedoch mehr denn je mit vielen Fragezeichen und Ungewissheiten versehen. Ungewissheit über Begriffe, Definitionen und auch über konkrete Ausformungen eigener „alternativer" Lösungsansätze.

Warum eigentlich?

Was genau ist in den Jahrzehnten nach dem Zusammenbruch des Ostblocks passiert, das uns veranlasst unsere bisherigen Ansätze kritisch zu reflektieren?

Zunächst einmal gilt wohl, dass es weltweit nach wie vor kein islamisches Vorzeigemodell gab und gibt, das den eigenen Anspruch hinsichtlich eines alternativen Gesellschaftsmodells ausreichend untermauert. Selbst da, wo Gestaltungsmöglichkeiten insbesondere in Form von Regierungsverantwortung möglich wurden, offenbarte sich eine erhebliche Diskrepanz zwischen Anspruch und Wirklichkeit der Konzepte.

Darüberhinaus hat der unaufhaltsame Siegeszug des als „Globalisierung" daherkommenden ungezügelten Kapitalismus auch am Selbstverständnis der Muslime gerüttelt.

Was bis Mitte der neunziger Jahre noch als Auseinandersetzung auf Augenhöhe verstanden wurde, geriert sich aus Sicht der Muslime im Lichte eines als maßlos empfundenen Überlegenheitsanspruches, insbesondere mit dem ausgerufenen weltweiten Krieg gegen den sogenannten „islamisch" motivierten Terrorismus, immer mehr als Kampf einer überlegenen Zivilisation gegenüber „rückständigen" Zivilisationen.

Als in Europa lebende Muslime bleiben auch wir von den Folgen dieser weltweiten Auseinandersetzungen nicht verschont. Immer häufiger und lauter fragen wir uns, ob wir tatsächlich „neue Antworten" in unseren Quellen suchen oder vielmehr als Folge unserer Sozialisation im europäischen Kontext, aber auch aufgrund des gesellschaftlichen Anpassungsdruckes der auf Muslimen in Europa besonders lastet, die Antworten, die von uns gewünscht oder gefordert werden, schon längst wissen und versuchen diese „religiös abzusegnen".

Egal um welche Themenstellung es geht, ob Demokratie, Menschenrechte, Verfassung, Marktwirtschaft, Freiheit, Geschlechtergleichheit: wie selbstverständlich spulen wir „Bekenntnisformeln" als Muslime ab und sehen natürlich auch keinen Widerspruch zu den unseren eigenen Quellen.

Die Liste kann dann auch beliebig fortgeführt werden. Gegen dieses veränderte Religionsverständnis, das seinen Niederschlag natürlich auch in unserem Verband findet, regt sich in der eigenen Gemeinschaft, aber auch unter muslimischen Intellektuellen außerhalb Europas teilweise erbitterter Widerstand.

Widerstand gegen ein als allzu unterwürfig empfundenes Islam- Verständnis. Dabei gilt jedes neue Bekenntnis zu westlichen Konzepten und die quasi-religiöse Absegnung derselbigen als verzweifelter Versuch, dem obsiegenden westlichen Wertesystem eine islamische Legitimation zu verschaffen.

Innergemeindliche Spannungen sind bei den aufeinanderprallenden Vorstellungen vorprogrammiert. Und schnell fallen dann auch Begriffe wie „Euro-Islam" oder „Moderater Islam", die Inbegriffe „imperialistischer Unterwerfungskonzeptionen", die zum Ziel haben, dem Islam seinen Gestaltungsanspruch als gesellschaftliche Alternative auszutreiben. Entsprechend groß ist die Skepsis, die insbesondere der jungen Funktionärsgeneration in unserem Verband entgegen schlägt. Schnell werden die immer wieder eingeforderten Debatten um die inhaltliche und thematische Neuausrichtung in den Kontext der vorgenannten Schlagwörter und Auseinandersetzungen gestellt.

Der Schlüsselbegriff, der wohl die Situation, in der wir uns als Verantwortliche befinden, am besten zusammenfasst, lautet „Misstrauensdiskurs". Und als ob der „Misstrauensdiskurs" in den eigenen Reihen nicht reichen würde, macht uns darüberhinaus die s.g. „Mehrheitsgesellschaft" mit ihrer vom globalen Terrorismus geprägten Erwartungshaltung gegenüber Muslimen das Leben schwer. Was wir nicht alles machen müssen, um unseren Platz in der Gesellschaft als Gleicher unter Gleichen einzunehmen. Den Koran historisieren, uns vom Cihad distanzieren, das Kopftuch ablegen, jeglicher Politisierung des Glaubens abschwören, uns also mit Lichtgeschwindigkeit in die Postmoderne katapultieren.

Wie auch der das Thema dieses Symposiums verdeutlicht, sind viele Dinge ins Schwimmen geraten und sie sind nicht einfach in die Kategorien „schwarz" und „weiß" einzuordnen, wie ich das in meinem Vortrag zugegebenermaßen mit einem gewissen Hang zur Überspitzung getan habe.

In einem solchen Spannungsfeld kann es eine ernsthafte Verbandsführung nicht allen gleichermaßen Recht machen. Was wir auf jeden Fall nicht machen werden, ist unsere Unterschrift unter vorgefertigte „europakompatible" Konzepte zu setzen, die man uns, ohne auf unsere inhaltliche Mitwirkung überhaupt Wert zu legen, überstülpen will.

Genauso wenig lassen wir uns Diffamierungen unseres Ansatzes gefallen und werden auch unsere bisherigen Konzepte nicht auf den Prüfstein stellen, weil die Würdigung eines sich verändernden Lebensrahmens oder gesellschaftlichen Kontextes zu den ureigenen Dynamiken islamischer Theologie gehört.

Es muss nicht schmerzlich sein, sich einzugestehen, dass man auf der Suche nach vermeintlich islamischen Antworten auf gesellschaftliche Grundsatzfragen erkennt, dass bewährte Konzepte wie Demokratie oder soziale Marktwirtschaft dem eigenen Ideal von einem auf Gerechtigkeit fußendem System am nächsten kommen, ohne dass sie gemeinhin als „islamische" Konzeptionen gelten. Das schmälert weder die Bedeutung unserer Religion, noch kann es uns davon abhalten, im Lichte unserer religiösen, kulturellen und also zivilisatorischen Wurzeln unseren gesellschaftlichen Gestaltungsanspruch mit Werten wie Brüderlichkeit, Solidarität, Mitgefühl und Barmherzigkeit aufrecht zu erhalten.

Comment

Massoud Shadjareh (England)

First of all, I would like to thank the organizers, Millî Görüş, for giving me this opportunity to come here and to enjoy participating in the wonderful conference and discussion. I have to say that unfortunately I agree with much of what has already been said. I think that Millî Görüş is facing what has repeatedly been seen in many similar organizations throughout Europe. In Britain, it is similar with the notable difference that a majority of its Muslims belong to the Indo-Pak Asian community. Indeed, they are a backbone in wealth creation for Britain in a similar manner to how the Turkish community has contributed to the general prosperity of modern Germany.

I think the case is quite clear. When the first generation settled in Europe, they set up the mosques and a halal meat industry, necessities at that time. The challenge is, now, what other institutions are going to be needed and how we, as Muslims, living within Europe should address those needs. It is very interesting because the things that you mentioned, especially the fall of communism, have had a tremendous impact. We were writing article after article at that time saying that NATO needed to be organized to fight Muslim terrorism and Muslim fundamentalism. At that time, I was wondering what this was all about. I, as most of us, at that time did not realize what was brewing.

Another event which had a tremendous resonance with Muslims in Europe was the tragic conflict in Bosnia Herzegovina. It was profoundly shocking to witness, in our modern times, a religious community massacred in the streets of Europe. Something not seen or even imagined possible since the end of the Nazis era, we saw again that same mentality, now euphemistically referred to as "ethnic cleansing" rather than "genocide," taking place in the streets of Europe... So much of Europe seemed completely indifferent to it. When one quotes from President Clinton's memoirs, he actually states in his own words, "We couldn't get involved in challenging the massacre because Europe did not want to have an Islamic entity within it." This was very clearly being said. This has had a tremendous impact on the psyche of the Muslims.

Yet, now, we see that demonization process continues. In fact, recently I saw the name of Millî Görüş and similar organizations highlighted within a report from the intelligence services. This is not different from what is now happening in Britain. Something happened a few months ago, which shocked me. I was in a meeting of so-called intelligence experts from all around Europe, talking about the threat of terrorism. Two German experts stood up and made a comment that in one city, I do not remember which city it was, there were 25 to 30 thousand extremists who were viable to become terrorists. I raised my hands up and queried, "Well, this is very interesting but how did you come to this conclusion? I mean, what have they done that you actually categorize them that way?" To my shock and surprise, the guy replied saying, "Well, these are the guys who don't want their daughters to attend mixed swimming." I was so shocked that I didn't know how to respond to this. So, not wanting your daughters to go to mixed swimming or your children to go to mixed swimming somehow implies you are fanatical and a potential terrorist!

These are realities that are all happening there, and all of us need to deal with it. The politics of fear which has been created has become a real thing. Last year, Europol reported that there had been 500 terrorist attacks within

Europe. Now here comes the question: "How many of them were motivated and done by Muslims?" One! Only one! But that is not the perception which is created outside. Even in England, unfortunately we had to go through 7/7 [refers to 7 July 2005 London bombings, *e.g.*] and other kind of terrorist activities. It is much more statistically probable for myself and any of my fellow countrymen to die as a victim of medical malpractice at a local hospital than as a result of terrorism. That is to say, when viewed from the perspective of a sober, balanced, rational and statistically realistic assessment of all such plausible potential risks, why is nobody declaring war on these more plausible dangers to society with a greater enthusiasm proportional to risk? How come people are not terrified of visiting the hospital, compared to say boarding a plane? How and why has such a distorted sense fear been induced in people's consciousness? Research conducted in the United States, suggests some 80 percent of Americans are fearful of becoming victims of terrorism. While similar polling undertaken in Iraq revealed that, despite the fact that the conflict claims about fifty lives on a daily basis, the general population do not display that same level of personal anxiety. So why is this? Obviously, this is a consequence of "Politics of Fear" which, is a historically well-known phenomenon, and I should also point out that it is not simply just us, Muslims who are its victims but rather, indeed, the wider community at large. It is a travesty that society is subjected to live in this kind of constant fear merely as a divisive political control mechanism. We thus need to actually expose this, and I think what we need to do in the future is actually to work harder than we have so far to get the message out. And I know Millî Görüş is one of the best run Muslim organizations in Germany. However, we still actually need to get out and do more work to counteract this false perception that has been created.

We need to cultivate Muslims who are confident and articulate. We also need to go out and build confidence within our communities, our youth, and our wider community at large. Not the type of confidence that comes across as arrogance because that would be counterproductive. We do not need arrogant people; we want to be both confident and also humble. We need to move forward, organize networking with other Muslim organizations; not only in our neighbourhood, but widely across Europe. We need to do this. This is a must for us because our future is actually interlocked.

We heard so many different accusations and the exposure of false terminology. Let me bring in another one: the issue of enlightenment. You cannot have enlightenment unless you have dark ages because enlightenment comes out of dark ages. Dark ages have nothing to do with Muslims and Islam. It is something that is a peculiar characteristic to Christian history. The more we, Muslims, go back, the more there is light. You go closer to the Prophet (saws), you see more light and more guidance. So, we do not have this experience of enlightenment. We need to grasp the right terminology to explain. Muslims and Islam have been doing this all the time. We also need to be confident in use of our own terminology and construct our own intellectual framework to use it effectively.

I want to add to this. I saw a well-known Zionist give a speech in Tel Aviv recently; his tone was rather disturbing. He said that we are either going to have a European Islam or Islamic Europe. He went on to stoke an exaggerated fear that because of the demography and the fact that Muslims have more children etc., they are going to become very powerful within the European nation. Their influence is going to be powerful. He proposed that organizations such as Mossad should actually identify leaderships, which are to the detriment of the interest of the Zionist community, and deliberately and maliciously organize activities to frame, discredit and remove them from the leadership. This is both very worrying and disturbing and I think this should be of concern not just for Muslims, but also for all civil society institutions. Here, an external foreign power is overtly discussing the manipulation of European leadership, of the European way of moving forward. We need to identify and expose such attitudes and activities.

But more than anything, we actually need institutions to deal with attacks against our community. In Britain, today with a population of about 1.8 million Muslims yet we have only one caseworker dealing with cases of attacks against Muslims. This is an unacceptable situation. I am not familiar with the equivalent position in Germany, France or elsewhere in Europe. We need to create such institutions to protect us. That is something we need to work together for. I really believe that the experience gained of "how to create these institutions" needs to be shared between our communities. We need to promote the concept of Islam. Some people suggest that according to *fiqh*, we, Muslims, on the basis of possessing our passports, have given allegiance to our respective governments. But taking that argument to its absurd conclusion would have meant that someone who lived in Germany and was German, during the era of the Nazis and the 3rd Reich, would have had to have given allegiance to the Nazis and all they perpetrated. This is absurd. We should give our allegiance to truth and justice, we give allegiance to the right way forward and we give allegiance to what is right and righteous. From that point of view, we are committed as Muslims to fostering a better and just society for all that all of society will benefit from. This is the message that needs to be put out. It needs to go out to all citizens of Europe. What we want is a better society for all of us. We want to have a share in that. We want to create that society collectively with Muslims and non-Muslims.

Assalamu alaikum wa rahmatullah.

Kurzbiographien der ReferentInnen

Yavuz Celik Karahan

Yavuz Çelik Karahan kam 1956 in der türkischen Stadt Kırşehir zur Welt. Nach dem Imam-Hatip-Gymnasium studierte er Literaturwissenschaft an der Universität Konya. Nach einer Zeit als Vorsitzender des Regionalverbands Frankreich sowie als Vorsitzender der Jugendorganisation wurde Karahan 2003 zum Vorsitzenden der Islamischen Gemeinschaft Millî Görüş (IGMG) gewählt. Karahan übte das Amt des Vorsitzenden bis 2011 aus.

Dr. Mustafa Cerić

Dr. Mustafa Cerić ist ein bosnischer Islamgelehrter. Bis November 2012 war Cerić Großmufti von Bosnien und Herzegowina. Seit 29. Dezember 2012 ist Cerić Präsident des Bosniakischen Weltkongresses und Mitgründer der Bosniakischen Akademie der Wissenschaften und Künste. Er studierte von 1974 bis 1978 an der Kairoer Al-Azhar-Universität Theologie und Philosophie. 1987 promovierte er bei Fazlur Rahman an der University of Chicago über die Theologie Abu Mansur al-Maturidis.

Dr. Syed Farid Alatas

Dr. Syed Farid Alatas ist Leiter des Fachbereichs für Malaiische Studien sowie Associate Professor am Fachbereich Soziologie der National University of Singapore. Er ist malaiischer Staatsbürger, erhielt seine Schulbildung jedoch in Singapur. 1991 erlangte Alatas an der Johns Hopkins University (USA) seinen PhD in Soziologie. Bis zu seiner Berufung

an die National University of Singapore im Jahre 1992 lehrte
er an der Fakultät Südostasien-Studien der University of Malaya.

Dr. Parvez Manzoor

Dr. Parvez Manzoor wurde in Pakistan geboren und lebt
seit 1963 in Schweden. Er ist Herausgeber der Internetzeitschrift Islam21 (London) sowie des Muslim World Book
Review (Leicester, Großbritannien). Vorher war er unter
anderem Vorsitzender der Schwedisch-Muslimischen Föderation, Herausgeber des Afkar-Inquiry (London) sowie
Gastprofessor an der International Islamic University in
Malaysia. Sowohl im Westen als auch in der islamischen
Welt wurde Parvez Manzoor vor allem bekannt durch seine
zahlreichen Beiträge zu gegenwärtigen Debatten über den
Islam. Einige seiner Schriften wurden ins Arabische, Türkische, Malaiische, Indonesische, Chinesische u.v.a. Sprachen
übersetzt. Sie sind zum Teil verfügbar auf der Internetseite
www.pmanzoor.info.

Amr G. E. Sabet

Amr G. E. Sabet ist Politikwissenschaftler aus Kanada. Den
Schwerpunkt seiner Lehr- und Forschungstätigkeit bilden
die Gebiete der Internationalen Beziehungen, Vergleichenden Politik, der Politik des Mittleren Ostens und der
islamischen Politik. Er hat viel auf diesen Gebieten veröffentlicht und unterrichtet. Gegenwärtig ist er assoziierter
Professor für Politikwissenschaft an der Dalarna Universität
in Schweden. Zudem unterrichtet Amr Sabet an der Fakultät für Politikwissenschaft der Universität von Helsinki in
Finnland.

Prof. Dr. Ahmet Çiğdem

Prof. Dr. Ahmet Çiğdem wurde 1964 im türkischen Çankırı
geboren. Derzeit ist er als der Dozent für Soziologie an der
ODTÜ tätig, wo er bereits seinen Masterabschluss erwarb
und anschließend promovierte. Er hat wissenschaftliche

Arbeiten mit Schwerpunkt auf den Gebieten Moderne, Islam, Türkei sowie Religiosität verfasst und befasst sich zur Zeit mit dem Themenbereich Hegel, Deutscher Idealismus, Religion und Islamismus. Folgende Bücher wurden von ihm publiziert: Akıl ve Toplumun Özgürleşimi (Vadi, 1992; İletişim, 2008); Aydınlanma Düşüncesi (Ağaç, 1993; İletişim, 1997); Bir İmkân Olarak Modernite (İletişim, 1997); Taşra Epiği (Birikim, 2001), Toplum: Kavram ve Gerçeklik (İletişim, 2006), D'nin Hâlleri: Din, Darbe, Demokrasi (İletişim, 2009), Geleceği Eskitmek: AKP ve Türkiye (İletişim, 2014).

Prof. Dr. Stefano Allievi

Prof. Dr. Stefano Allievi wurde 1958 in Mailand/Italien geboren. Er studierte bis 1992 in Trento Politische Wissenschaften und erlangte 1997 an der Fakultät für Soziologie den den Grad eines Doktors der Philosophie. Seīt 1998 lehrt er an der Universität Padova als außerordentlicher Professor für Soziologie im Master-Studiengang für Kommunikationswissenschaften. Von 2001 bis 2007 war er Sekretär der Abteilung für Religionssoziologie der italienischen Gesellschaft für Soziologie (AIS). Seit 2013 ist er Präsident des Master-Studiengangs für Soziologie. Er spezialisierte sich auf Studien zur Migration, auf Religionssoziologie, auf den kulturellen Wandel in Europa unter besonderer Berücksichtigung des kulturellen und religiösen Pluralismus, und hier besonders der Präsenz des Islams.

Prof. Dr. Kadir Canatan

Prof. Dr. Kadir Canatan wurde im türkischen Nevşehir-Hacıbektaş geboren. An der Rotterdamer Sozialakademie studierte er Sozialarbeit und an der dortigen Erasmus Universität Soziologie. An der Freien Universität Amsterdam absolvierte er schließlich einen Masterstudiengang in der Soziologie nicht-westlicher Gesellschaften und Kulturanthropologie. 1986 begann er an der Erasmus Universität in Rotterdam im Fach Soziologie seine Promotion mit dem Titel „Die Entwicklung der türkischstämmigen Nichtregierungsorganisationen in den Niederlanden". 2005 trat er eine Stelle als Lehrbeauftragter im Fach Soziologie an der Universität Balıkesir an. Zur Zeit arbeitet er an der Sabahattin Zaim Universität in Istanbul. Einige der zahlreichen Arbeiten Canatans, die sich vor allem auf Themen wie Minderheiten, Multikulturalität, Integration und Migration konzentrieren, sind folgende: „Aile Sosyolojisi" (hrsg.), „Beden Sosyolojisi" (hrsg.), „Mukaddime: Klasik Sosyal Bilimler Sözlüğü", „İbn Haldun Perspektifinden Bilgi Sosyolojisi" und „Avrupa'da Ulusal Azınlıklar: Hollanda-Friesland Örneği."

Dr. Salman Sayyid

Dr. Salman Sayyid lehrte bereits an den Universitäten von Manchester, East London und Salford. Er ist Autor des Buches "A Fundamental Fear" (2003) und Mitherausgeber des Bandes "A Postcolonial People" (2006). Zurzeit ist er Forschungsbeauftragter am Institut für Soziologie und Sozialpolitik der Universität Leeds, Großbritannien.

Dr. Jörn Thielmann

Dr. Jörn Thielmann wurde 1966 in Essen geboren. Von 1985 bis 1991 studierte er an der Julius-Maximilians-Universität Würzburg sowie an der Ruhr-Universität Bochum Orientalische Philologie, Islamwissenschaften, Philosophie und Rechtswissenschaften. Seine Promotion im Fach Islamwissenschaften schloss er im Jahre 2001 ebenfalls an der Ruhr-Universität Bochum ab. Er absolvierte Studien- und Forschungsaufenthalte an verschiedenen Institutionen in Deutschland, Ägypten, Großbritannien und Marokko. Seit Januar 2009 ist er der Geschäftsführer des Erlanger Zentrums für Islam und Recht in Europa EZIRE an der Friedrich-Alexander-Universität Erlangen-Nürnberg (www.ezire.uni-erlangen.de).

Oğuz Üçüncü

Oğuz Üçüncü wurde 1969 in Hamm/Westfalen geboren. Nach dem Abitur 1988 in Hamm studierte er an der Fachhochschule in Dortmund und erlangte 1994 seinen Abschluss als Diplom-Maschinenbauingenieur. Bereits 1986 war er Vorsitzender der Jugendgruppe des IGMG Ortsvereins Hamm-Pelkum, 1990 Mitglied des Regionalvorstandes Nord-Ruhr und 1992 Mitglied des Regionalvorstandes Ruhr-A, bis er 1993 Mitglied des IGMG-Jugendvorstandes wurde. Von 2002 bis 2014 war Üçüncü Generalsekretär der IGMG. Üçüncü ist türkischer Staatsbürger, verheiratet und Vater von drei Töchtern.

Massoud Shadjareh

Massoud Shadjareh ist ein langjähriger Menschenrechtsaktivist, dessen Engagement bis zu den Anti-Vietnamkriegs-Protesten an der UCAL Berkeley in den späten 1960er Jahren zurückgeht. 1971 zog Shadjareh nach Großbritannien und übte dort etwa fünfzehn Jahre lang verschiedene ehrenamtliche Tätigkeiten aus. 1997 gründete er mit mehreren anderen muslimischen Aktivisten, die an verschiedenen nationalen und internationalen Projekten mitwirkten, die Islamische Kommission für Menschenrechte (Islamic Human Rights Commission, IHRC). Die IHRC ist eine Kampagnen-, Forschungs- und Interessenorganisation mit Sitz in London. Shadjareh ist derzeit Vorsitzender der IHRC. Zugleich ist er Mitglied des Stop and Search Review Community Panels, welches sich dem Problem widmet, dass Angehörige von Minderheiten unverhältnismäßig oft von Polizisten angehalten und durchsucht werden. Shadjareh absolvierte ein Studium der Internationalen Beziehungen in Cambridge und London.